STEP BY STEP THROUGH THE OLD TESTAMENT

~ LEADER GUIDE ~

RICK MITCHELL

LifeWay Press®
Nashville, Tennessee

Revised 2000
Ninth printing December 2007

ISBN 9780767326209
Item 001116312
This book is the text for course CG-0104
in the subject area Bible Studies in the Christian Growth Study Plan.

Dewey Decimal Classification: 221
Subject Heading: BIBLE.OLD TESTAMENT

Cover Illustration: Stefano Vitale

About the Author:
Rick Mitchell is a graduate of the University of Alabama and the New Orleans Baptist Theological Seminary (MDiv). Rick became involved in small-group disciple making in 1984, and pastored for 20 years in Alabama, Louisiana, and Mississippi. He now serves as a bi-vocational minister and consultant to churches. Rick is employed as a corporate consultant doing leadership development, employee and executive assessment, and seminar development and training. He resides in Tuscaloosa, Alabama, with his wife, Carol, and their daughters, Jennifer and Rachel.

To order additional copies of this resource: write LifeWay Church Resources Customer Service; One LifeWay Plaza; Nashville, TN 37234-0113; FAX order to (615) 251-5933; call toll free 1-800-458-2772; e-mail to *orderentry@lifeway.com;* order online at *www.lifeway.com;* or visit the LifeWay Christian Store serving you.

Printed in the United States of America

LifeWay Church Resources
One LifeWay Plaza
Nashville, Tennessee 37234-0175

Table of Contents

LIFE Enrollment/Attendance

Course Title ____________________

Leader ____________________

Name	Session Date (Check Attendance)												
	1	**2**	**3**	**4**	**5**	**6**	**7**	**8**	**9**	**10**	**11**	**12**	**13**
1													
2													
3													
4													
5													
6													
7													
8													
9													
10													

* Report weekly attendance to your Discipleship Training Director or general secretary.

* * You have permission to reproduce this form for use with your LIFE course small group.

Introduction and Administrative Guide

SMALL-GROUP DISCIPLING

The Small-Group Discipling Process

Christian discipleship involves redirecting one's life in obedience to Christ so the disciple can follow Him and become like Him. A small group provides one of the best contexts for this to happen. The group relationship gives us insight as we learn. It provides support as we redirect our lives under the lordship of Christ. You will sign a covenant together to reinforce group accountability and support. The more disciples serve together, the better they can help one another become like Christ.

Size of Groups for Effective Learning

Jesus preached to large crowds, but He did most of His discipleship training with a group of 12. He was even more intimate with three of His disciples who would be key leaders in the early church. You need to provide a learning environment where God can do His best work in the lives of group members. Being in a small group makes it easier to ask questions, share personal experiences, and pray intimately with one another. Eight to ten members is the best size for a group of this nature. If more persons are interested in this study, provide for multiple groups in order to create the best possible learning environment.

A Word About Multiplication

The goal of our Christian discipleship is to make disciples who will make disciples (2 Tim. 2:2). Discipleship is not complete until the disciple is helping others to be disciples. As you lead the group, watch for persons who show potential for becoming leaders themselves. Give them opportunities to share in leading part of a session. If you must be gone, enlist one of these to serve as leader in your place.

Strive for quality instead of quantity. Starting small and growing is better than starting big and failing. Commit yourself to doing the kind of quality discipling that requires patience, hard work, accountability, and vision. The long-term benefit will be worth it. You will witness the infusion of renewed spiritual life and vitality into every area of the church as God grows and matures His people.

AN OVERVIEW OF *STEP BY STEP THROUGH THE OLD TESTAMENT*

For an introduction to the course, read the introduction in the member's book before you continue reading this overview.

Step by Step Through the Old Testament is a 13-session survey of the Old Testament Scriptures. The basic course goal is to offer adult Christians an overview of the 39 books of the Old Testament. However, *Step by Step Through the Old Testament* is not just a book for reading. It is part of a learning system designed to teach the content material and help people move into a deeper relationship with God.

Step by Step Through the Old Testament is a preparation for ministry course. It directly relates to the ministries of teaching and preaching, and will be a dynamic benefit to church leaders involved in the Bible study and member training programs of the church. Members will come away from the course with a broad grasp of the people, places, themes, and message of the Old Testament.

The LIFE Learning System

Step by Step Through the Old Testament and other LIFE courses are offered through the church's Discipleship Training. If your church does not have regular member training, you still can offer the course. In fact, some churches are using LIFE courses to start or revitalize their training of disciples through Discipleship Training. The Lay Institute for Equipping is a self-study system designed to equip adult Christians with knowledge and skills in basic ministry areas. The courses are taught using an interactive learning model. For maximum benefits, every element of the learning system should be utilized. Participants should complete each daily study on their own. They then meet weekly in a small group (eight to ten people maximum) to review, discuss questions that arise, share personal experiences and insights, and apply the truths to life. *Step by Step Through the Old Testament* is part of that system.

The Uniqueness of *Step by Step Through the Old Testament*

You can see the primary theme of *Step by Step Through the Old Testament* in the unit titles. God is the author, subject, and focal point of the Old Testament. This study will lead participants through a close examination of the major people, places, themes, and events in which God chose to reveal Himself. In this study, participants should experience God speaking to them personally in the literature of the Old Testament.

Step by Step Through the Old Testament is an overview course that offers a framework of knowledge for teachers and other leaders in the church as they seek to equip and lead God's people. Any Christian will benefit from studying *Step by Step Through the Old Testament.* But those who teach and lead Bible study make up the primary audience for this course. Pastors who need introductory training or simply want an intensive refresher course in Old Testament make up another target audience for this course.

How to Use This Guide

This leader's guide is designed to assist you in preparing for and conducting the small-group sessions each week. The following material will guide you in preparing for the course, enlisting participants, and preparing for the small-group sessions.

1. If you have not already done so, read thoroughly the introduction to the course in the member's book.
2. Next, finish reading the course administrative guide contained in this leader guide.
3. Using the instructions in this guide, make a list of and begin gathering necessary supplies and extra resources you may need.
4. Use a calendar to outline a tentative time frame for the course. Plan for a period of about 16 weeks.

GETTING GROUPS STARTED

Decide on the Number of Groups Needed

Work with the pastor, Discipleship Training director, or others to determine how many individuals in your church want to study this course at this time. Any adult who already has trusted Jesus Christ as Lord and Savior will benefit from this study. Survey your church membership to determine the number of persons interested in a study of the Old Testament. As mentioned earlier, you will need one group for every 10 to 12 members.

Order Resources

Necessary resources should be ordered for the course eight to ten weeks prior to the first session. Course materials may be ordered on the Undated Materials Order Form, or by calling LifeWay Christian Resources. Allow time for processing and shipping your order—remember that leaders need time to prepare for the introductory session and to enlist participants. Though you may not enlist participants until later, you can estimate the quantity needed by ordering eight to ten member books and one leader guide for each small group. Resources include:

- *Step by Step Through the Old Testament (Member book)* (ISBN 0-7673-2619-9)
- *Step by Step Through the Old Testament Leader Guide* (ISBN 0-7673-2620-2)

Orders or order inquiries may be sent to LifeWay Church Resources Customer Service; One LifeWay Plaza, Nashville, TN 37234-0113; FAX order to (615) 251-5933; phone 1-800-458-2772; e-mail to *CustomerService@lifeway.com;* ONLINE at *www.lifeway.com;* or visit the LifeWay Christian Store serving you.

A similar set of resources is available for *Step by Step Through the New Testament.*

- *Step by Step Through the New Testament (Member book)* (ISBN 0-8054-9946-6)
- *Step by Step Through the New Testament Leader Guide* (ISBN 0-7673-2621-0)

Enlist Leaders

Each group should have at least one leader. The primary role of leaders of *Step by Step Through the Old Testament* is that of facilitator. As such, they are to be role models and catalysts for learning. Pray that God will help you identify those persons that He wants to lead the groups. These leaders should be spiritually growing Christians and active church members. Leaders should have teachable spirits, ability to relate well to people, a commitment to keep confidential information private, and a willingness to spend the time necessary to prepare for the sessions.

Also look for people who possess skills for leading small-group learning experiences. They should be interested in developing disciples. Alumni of *MasterLife: Discipleship Training* could make excellent group leaders since they have experienced the discipling process. To sum up some of the requirements for leaders, they should

- be dedicated, faithful Christians.
- be role models in their knowledge and practice of Bible teachings.
- love people and enjoy helping them grow in Christ.

Explore with your pastor the possibility of his leading the first group. Having your pastor lead the first study offers several advantages.

- Pastoral leadership attaches importance to the study in the eyes of church members.
- The pastor's spiritual growth is enhanced.
- Leaders for future groups can be identified and benefit from the modeling done by the pastor as he leads the initial study.

Enlist Participants

Whom should you enlist? Here are some suggestions that will help you know where to look for prospective group members.

- Church leaders and church program teachers.
- New Christians who have completed *Survival Kit for New Christians.*
- Persons who have joined your church from other denominations.
- Members who want to grow in Christ.
- Potential leaders.
- MasterLife alumni.

How should you enlist group members? Use these suggestions as guidelines for enlistment efforts.

- Pray for God to lead you and them.
- Promote the course as you would other study opportunities.
- Make a personal contact before a person is enlisted as a group member. Sit down with the person and explain the expectations, requirements, anticipated results, and materials costs of the course.

What are the requirements? Each participant should have clear understanding of the following requirements.

- Individual study of about 30-60 minutes a day for five days a week. This will include memorizing at least one Scripture verse each week.
- Group Participation.
  -Attend the weekly group session.
  -Make up any session missed.
  -Encourage and support other group members.
  -Be accountable to the group for completion of weekly assignments.
  -Openly share in the group.
  -Pray for one another.
- Discipleship growth. Members are expected to want to grow as they progress through training.

What are some pitfalls to avoid? You will avoid problems by planning for the following situations.

- Not enough leaders for the number of members.
- Over enlistment. Let the maximum group size be known in case you are overrun with potential members.
- Agreeing to allow "observers" who want to just "sit in and listen." *Step by Step Through the Old Testament* is not a spectator Bible study. Decide how you will respond to those who want the knowledge without doing the work. Plan to encourage such persons to wait until a time when they can be a participant in the fullest sense.
- Trying to facilitate too many groups yourself. I know (from painful experience) that it is better to do a good job with one group than a poor job with several. However, you can facilitate two groups if you keep them on the same units. If you should lead two groups, schedule them at different times and on different days of the week.

Scheduling Sessions

Discipleship Training of this depth cannot be done well in less than one hour. Group sessions should last from 1 to 1½ hours. (Sessions are configured around 70 minutes or more being available. Adjust time as needed for shorter sessions). Groups may meet at the church, in homes, or other locations convenient to members. You may want to offer group studies at a variety of times and locations so more people will be able to participate. Consider these options:

- Sunday evening at church. Groups can meet prior to the evening worship service.
- Weekday evening at church. Groups can meet prior to or following the mid-week prayer service.
- Weekday morning, afternoon, or evening. Groups can meet in homes, at the church, or at work during a time most convenient to participants. One advantage to this option is the relaxed atmosphere. Participants will not be rushing to finish in order to go to a worship service as is the case in the first two options.

Split sessions are also a possibility. You could meet on Sunday night and again after worship services on Wednesday evening. You also could choose to extend the course from 14 to 28 sessions and study only one part of a unit each week. This will call for a long-term commitment on the part of participants, but the amount of required study each week will be reduced. If you choose to split the sessions, you will probably want to agree on additional readings in the Old Testament. Design your schedule to meet the needs of your people.

Discipleship groups may meet anytime and anyplace that is convenient for members. The process works best when meetings are in a home. Elaborate refreshments are not recommended lest they take too much of the members' preparation and group time.

If you choose to have only one hour per week for your group sessions, the following guidelines will help you adjust the structure of the course.

Recommended Choice: Take two weeks per unit of study.

- Complete individual study and use the first hour's agenda for the first group session.
- Encourage individual review of the unit during the second week and use the second hour's agenda for the second group session. This option would require a minimum of 27 weeks—an introductory session and 26 group sessions.

PREPARING TO LEAD THE STUDY

Suggestions in this section are directed to the persons who have been enlisted to serve as group leaders. Following these suggestions will help you make adequate preparation for carrying out your responsibilities and will help equip you to be an effective leader.

Your Role as a Small-group Leader

You may be asking yourself, "Why did I agree to lead this group? I need to know more about the Old Testament myself." If you sense God has led you to accept this assignment, you can trust Him to equip and enable you to accomplish the task. Your role in a small-group study is not that of a teacher. Rather, your responsibility is to facilitate the group learning process. The following guidelines are taken from *MasterBuilder: Multiplying Leaders*, and will help you facilitate the growth process with your group.

1. Create an atmosphere of acceptance and sharing. Room arrangement is essential to group atmosphere. Set up the room so that members are in a circle and within arm's reach of one another. Make sure the room is quiet and free of distractions.

2. Model the attitude of a servant. Members will take their cues from you. Ask God to help you balance the group leadership role with that of a servant to the group.

3. Participate as a group member. Be a part of the process. Allow God to lead the group. You often will find that once the discussion is started, the Lord will gently lead it along and make the truths relevant to the group.

4. Involve all group members in the discussion. "As iron sharpens iron, so one man sharpens another" (Prov. 27:17). Find ways to involve members who are hesitant to participate without embarrassing them or forcing them to be more open to the group than they are willing to be. As the members grow in their knowledge so they will grow in their ability to get into the group interaction. The truths of the Scripture will come into focus as the members test and dig into the ideas. Do not allow any member to habitually adopt the role of critic. Encourage all the members to take part.

5. Keep the group moving toward its goals. Keeping the group on track and moving toward achieving the learning goal is important. There will be times when you will have to encourage the group to get back on track or to move on in their discussion.

Prepare or Secure Additional Resources

Much of your course preparation can be completed at one time. Everything you can do before the study begins will free time later for personal and spiritual preparation. Pages 57-63 contain materials to be used during the group sessions. At the appropriate time, you will be instructed to make copies of these materials for use in the sessions. Some of the material is optional and you may or may not choose to use it. Pages 13-56 provide step-by-step directions for leading an introductory session and 13 group sessions based on members' individual study during the previous week.

1. Duplicated materials. Make copies of the following pages in this leader's guide for group members. Some are optional or may be prepared on a poster or chalkboard, so use your own judgment. You have permission to copy the following pages, but only for use with groups studying *Step by Step Through the Old Testament*.

Highly Recommended:
- Unit Review Quizzes (pp. 57-63)
- Scripture Memory Cards (p. 64) If possible, use heavier card stock for the Scripture Memory Cards or paste them on card stock after copying.

2. Prepare a *Memorizing Scripture* poster. Turn to "Help Members Memorize Scripture" (p. 11). Write the boldface instructions or key words on a poster for use in the introductory and first small-group sessions.

3. Provide markerboard or large sheets of paper and markers for use throughout the course. Keep a supply readily available.

4. Obtain a good set of Bible maps for use in the group sessions. If your church does not own a set, see whether you can borrow them from your associational office or Discipleship Training Director. They also may be ordered from LifeWay® Christian Stores (call 1-800-233-1123). Make certain you also obtain an easel on which to mount the maps.

Anticipate Difficult Questions

The Old Testament is not as familiar to most Christians as the New. Expect questions you may not be able to answer. Encourage participants to join you in praying and searching the Scriptures. Together, ask God to guide you to His answer. Just as God spoke to His people through the Old Testament, He will speak to you. When God answers through one or more group members, you all will know more of God through experience. Here is a vital rule for any group facilitator: you best help your members when you equip them to find their own answers.

As the group facilitator, you may want to obtain some additional study resources to aid you in your preparation. Studying the complete text before making any purchases will help ensure that you purchase those resources that will be most helpful to you.

Suggested Resources:

Hester, H. I. *The Heart of Hebrew History*, Broadman Press.

Cate, Robert L. *An Introduction to the Old Testament and Its Study*, Broadman Press.

The Biblical Illustrator, published quarterly by LifeWay Christian Resources of the Southern Baptist Convention. This periodical contains concise articles about cultural, historical, and biblical subjects related to the quarterly Sunday School lessons. You'll find excellent material to supplement your study in *Step by Step Through the Old Testament*.

CONDUCTING SESSIONS

Understand How the Group Session Plans Are Structured

Give careful preparation to the weekly group session. This will be the time when the group will "pull it all together" and apply the truth of the Scriptures to their lives. Each group-session plan includes three parts: Before the Session, During the Session, and After the Session. Let's look more closely at each of these major divisions.

Before the Session. This section includes actions for you to complete prior to the group session. Boxes are provided for you to check as you complete each action. I have done my best to provide sessions that require a minimum of leader preparation. If you adapt the lesson plans or create activities of your own, you will need to secure any resources that are required for these activities. Most of the units will have an optional learning activity to reinforce some aspect of the content. Decide at the time you do the "Before the Session" preparation if you will do the optional identification activities for that particular unit.

During the Session. This section provides questions and learning activities for use in conducting a two-hour group session. The activities follow a similar pattern each week. The first hour reviews the content of the unit members studied during the previous week. The second hour focuses on discussion and assimilation of the biblical content.

Each session concludes with a prayer time, followed by a preview of the next unit.

Here is what a session schedule should look like.

***Part 1* (30-45 minutes)**

1. **Group Time**
   This time allows members to relax and share what they have been experiencing.
2. **Review Time**
   During this segment members have a unit review quiz which calls for them to review or recall key people, places, ideas, dates, and Scripture passages from the unit content they studied during the previous week. Answers to the review quiz for each week are given in the training plan for that week.

Break (5 minutes)

***Part 2* (30-45 minutes)**

3. **Bible Study and Group Discussion**
   Discussion, check-up, and affective learning activities will help members understand and apply the session content.
4. **Preview Next Week's Assignment**
   Content and activities for the following week will be introduced, interest will be generated for the coming unit, and prayer will be offered.

After the Session. This section guides you in evaluating the group session, your performance as a leader, and the needs of group members. It is intended to help you constantly improve your abilities to guide the group members in their learning and spiritual growth. Each week you are encouraged to pray for your group members and identify one or more who may need a personal contact from you. I hope you will not neglect this aspect of your ministry. Your primary assignment in this study is to help people grow in Christ, not just teach knowledge. Remember, disciple making is investing your life in others!

Coping with Problems[1]

*1. **Members who are absent***. Ask members to tell you before the session if they will be absent. If they do not, contact them as soon as possible after the session. Arrange to meet them for a make-up session. Do not let them get two or three weeks behind, or they probably will drop out.

*2. **Members who do not complete their homework***. Expect homework assignments to be completed using an honor system. You might want to ask persons who have not completed assignments related to the topic under discussion not to ask questions during that portion of the session. Meet privately with individuals who are struggling to encourage them to remain current. Help them resolve problems they may be experiencing. They cannot receive the benefit of *Step by Step Through the Old Testament* if they do not do their study. If the problem persists, suggest that perhaps this is not the right time for them to complete the course, and that they withdraw until a later time. This sounds harsh. However, if they do not do their work, they will hurt the spirit and motivation of the entire group.

*3. **Members who want to drop out.*** Many times they have not studied seriously for years and are out of the habit. Do what you can to encourage them to stick with the course and manage their time better. If they must drop out, do not make them feel guilty. Encourage them to look for an opportunity to complete the course at a later date.

*4. **Members who do not agree with the content.*** Some debate in the group is good. The Scriptures always should be the final source of authority. If debate becomes counter productive, you may just say, "Why don't you and I get together and discuss this later? Our time is limited here and others also want to ask questions." This will defuse a possible disagreement and allow you to complete the group session.

*5. **Members who dominate the group.*** As the leader, make sure every person gets an opportunity to share. You may discourage dominating members by calling on other persons, asking that someone who has not spoken yet answer the next question, focusing your attention on someone else, and so forth. Some groups may take care of the problem themselves by their reactions to the dominating person. If those methods do not work, talk privately with the person who is dominating. Ask that person's help in getting everyone to participate in the discussion. As a last resort, state the problem candidly and ask for his/her cooperation.

Context- verses coming before or After memory verse
the Circumstances in which an event occurs

6. Not enough time in the session. Start and stop on time. Keep the group moving toward ending the session on schedule. Be punctual so members can pick up children and meet other engagements. If insufficient time is a persistent problem, the group may need to negotiate a longer session time if you are using less than 1½ hours.

7. Refreshments can be a problem. Keep refreshments simple. Do not allow persons to try to outdo one another. Make coffee and soft drinks available. Do not let the brief break in the middle of the session get out of hand. It is better to fellowship before or after the session.

8. Provisions for child care. If the group meets at the church during the Discipleship Training time, training should be provided for children and youth using recommended Discipleship Training resources. However, you may need to get someone to come early if you have 1½-hour sessions. If you meet at another time, members may pay for a baby sitter. Another church member may volunteer to care for the children this quarter, in turn for your getting someone to take care of his or her children next quarter. Sometimes the church will provide child care.

Set and Collect Fees

Group members should be expected to pay for the cost of materials. Your church may want to share the cost, but members should share some part of the expense. (I have found in years of working with LIFE courses, that not one person has ever lost a book he/she paid for.) Announce the fee at the time you enlist participants so they will not be embarrassed or surprised at the introductory session. You may want to provide some type scholarship for those who would need assistance.

STAYING ON TRACK

Keep Records

Work with the Discipleship Training director or general secretary to determine the best way of keeping enrollment and attendance records. Participation in a LIFE course such as *Step by Step Through the Old Testament* counts toward Discipleship Training participation regardless of the time of week it is offered. Report your weekly attendance to the Discipleship Training director or secretary. If your church does not have an ongoing Discipleship Training program, you can still count participation in *Step by Step Through the Old Testament* on the Discipleship Training section of the Annual Church Profile.

The church study course is another reason to keep a record of participation. Persons who complete the individual study of *Step by Step Through the Old Testament* and attend the group sessions qualify for the course diploma. These diplomas recognize the significant work of the participant.

Help Members Memorize Scripture[2]

Some of your group members may not be skilled at memorizing Scripture. The following suggestions may be helpful. Write the **boldface** instructions on a poster for use in the introductory and first small-group session. Be prepared to explain each of the suggestions.

1. Write verse and reference on a three-by-five-inch card. Include the topic and reference on the card.

2. Seek Understanding. Read the verse in its context. For instance, for John 15:5 you might read John 15:1-17. Study the verse and try to understand what it means. Read the verse aloud several times. Make certain you have "caught the sense" of what is being said. Read the verse in several translations until you can tell someone in your own words what it means.

3. Learn to quote the verse one phrase at a time. Divide the verse into short and meaningful phrases. Learn to quote the first phrase word for word. Then build on it by learning the second phrase. Continue until you are able to quote the entire verse word for word.

4. Quote the verse to another person. Ask him to check your accuracy.

5. Review the memorized verse regularly. During the first week, carry the card in your pocket or purse. Pull it out for review several times daily during waiting periods such as when riding an elevator, riding to work, or taking a coffee or lunch break. Review the verse at least daily for the first six weeks. Review weekly for the next six weeks and monthly thereafter.

Evaluate the Group Sessions[3]

Use the following questions to evaluate each group session. Make notes to jog your memory the next time you lead a group through this study.

1. Do you believe members achieved the session learning goals? Why or why not?
2. Did you dominate the discussion, or did you serve as a facilitator to involve members in the discussion?
3. Was everyone involved in learning activities? Do not force shy members, but encourage all to participate.
4. Did you show a genuine interest in each member of the group? What could have been done to create more interest and participation?
5. Did the session move smoothly and orderly?
6. What did you learn from the session that you should remember and use as you plan for the next session?
7. Do you need to make any personal contacts to encourage members of the group?

A Testimony of God's Leadership

In February of 1986 I realized the focus of His call to vocational ministry was for me to be an equipper. Since that time, the Lord has shown me again and again the highest service a pastor can render the church is to equip it to function as the body of Christ. I have gradually become committed to leading the church from what is known as a discipleship base.

No higher calling exists than communicating the gospel of Jesus Christ to those around us—whether it is in vocational ministry or in the daily marketplace. As for me, I am a pastor. In addition to a definite sense of call from God, pastoral work requires two gifts—the ability to relate to people and to communicate the message of the gospel.

This leader guide is a new aspect in communications for me. It is not an effort to communicate the gospel to you as much as it is a tool to help you equip the body of Christ. When properly equipped, the body can effectively communicate the gospel. In terms of writing, it is a first effort. The mistakes are mine. There is no claim for originality. The ideas are taken from sources I have heard or been exposed to in the past—most of which I cannot remember, but for which I am nonetheless grateful and indebted.

I have drawn heavily on the leader guide from several previous LIFE courses in writing this one. Specifically, I have used (with permission) material from *DecisionTime: Commitment Counseling, Experiencing God: Knowing and Doing the Will of God,* and *LifeGuide to Discipleship and Doctrine*. Seven years of involvement in *MasterLife* will be evident in what you see. My gratitude is herein expressed to Avery Willis and Claude King for their confidence in offering me this opportunity, and for their encouragement along the way to completion.

Additionally, the following persons gave invaluable assistance in the task. Our church secretary, Mrs. Terry Bufkin, accomplished a significant feat of data entry. Three colaborers and colleagues in the ministry, Tim Glaze, Larry Goff, and Mark Pinkerton, read the drafts and offered helpful comments. The church I presently serve, the Hickory Baptist Church of Hickory, Mississippi, has enthusiastically covenanted with me in small-group disciple making. As the session outlines were developed, two small groups of dedicated people in the church field tested the leader guides and member materials with me. Their faithfulness, patience, and hard work have helped produce a leader guide that is practical and useful in the church.

Finally, no leader guide can fully prepare you to facilitate a discipleship group. However, as you give yourself to prayerful and diligent study, God will honor the preparation and equip you for the work. I offer this guide with the prayer it will be used to give you assistance as you strive to "equip God's people for the work of the ministry."

---

[1]Adapted from Avery Willis, Jr., *LifeGuide to Discipleship and Doctrine Leader's Guide* (Nashville: Baptist Sunday School Board, 1989), 9-10.

[2]Adapted from Claude V. King, *Experiencing God Leader's Guide* (Nashville: LifeWay Press, 1990), 9-10.

[3]Adapted from Arthur H. Criscoe, Leonard Sanderson, *DecisionTime:Commitment Counseling* (Nashville: LifeWay Press, 1989), 266.

Introducing Step by Step Through the Old Testament

SESSION GOALS

In this session members will:

1. Be introduced to the course *Step by Step Through the Old Testament.*
2. Understand the requirements of the course.
3. Make a commitment to complete this study of the Old Testament.

Before the Session

❑ 1. Study the course Administrative Plan, and review the session goals.

❑ 2. Pray for God's guidance as you prepare. Specifically pray for those who will be present.

❑ 3. Read through "During the Session." Decide on the amount of time to allow for each segment of the Bible study. Write in the margin the time you want each segment to begin.

❑ 4. Gather or prepare the following materials:
- Copies of *Step by Step Through the Old Testament* for all participants.
- Prepare copies of the activity worksheet on page 15 to distribute at the end of the session.

❑ 5. Learn the unit 1 memory verse so you can share it when making assignments at the conclusion of this session.

❑ 6. If you have not already done so, prepare the poster to help members memorize Scripture (see page 11).

During the Session

OPENING ACTIVITIES (20 MINUTES)

1. Opening: Welcome everyone. If the participants do not know each other, make sure each has a name tag.

2. Spend a few minutes making introductions and becoming acquainted with group members.

3. Give each person a three-by-five-inch card or a small piece of paper and give these instructions:

   a. Record the location of the most memorable trip you ever took.

   b. Record the junk food you most likely would choose in a convenience store.

4. Collect the cards when everyone has finished. Read aloud the notations on the cards and have members try to identify the person who wrote the card.

Explain How the Course Works:
1. Introduce members to the interactive learning workbook. Emphasize the importance of doing the work each day and week. Explain that members will want to discipline themselves to spend time daily in meeting God through the pages of the Old Testament. Encourage them to begin now with a commitment to do each day's work as it comes. Ask members to discuss their commitment to a personal quiet time.

2. Group Sessions. The group sessions are part of the course requirements. Members will want to make certain they have the time to attend the group sessions before signing up for this course.

Introduce Step by Step Through the Old Testament.
Say, Our study of the Old Testament in *Step by Step Through the Old Testament* will be an exciting journey into the lives of the Old Testament people of God. The purpose of the course will be for you to experience God through the pages of the Old Testament.

Hand Out Materials:

1. Give each person a copy of *Step by Step Through the Old Testament*. Point out the unit pages that begin each unit. Ask members to scan the introductory statements to find a unit they think will be of particular interest to them.

2. Ask several members to share the units they selected and why. Encourage them to share what they want to get out of this study of the Old Testament.

3. Discuss the poster entitled "Memorizing Scripture." Quote the verse you learned as an example for the group.

4. Hand out the Activity Worksheet. Go over the instructions with the members. This activity will help them gain a renewed appreciation for the Scriptures, and particularly for the faithful people God used to preserve them down through the years.

CONCLUSION (10 MINUTES)

1. Preview next week's materials. Note that the next session's content will be a survey of the people and places of Palestine.

2. Point out the group covenant in the member's book. Tell members that in the next session they will be asked to sign one another's covenants as part of the course.

3. Remind members of the time and place of the group session.

4. Pray together.

After the Session

1. Carefully evaluate the effectiveness of the session.

    - Do you believe members satisfactorily achieved the session learning goals?

    - Did you dominate the discussion, or did you serve as a facilitator to involve members in the discussion?

    - Were all members involved in the learning activities?

    - Did you show a genuine interest in each member of the group? What could have been done to create more interest and participation?

    - Did the session move smoothly and orderly?

2. What did you learn from the session that you should remember and use as you plan for the next session?

3. Do you need to make any personal contacts to encourage members of the group?

4. Save any materials you have developed for use in future groups of *Step by Step Through the Old Testament*.

5. Immediately begin your preparation for next week's session. Make certain you have learned the memory verses.

6. Pray for the group. This week you should pray for their understanding that God has used human instruments to deliver His authoritative Word to us.

Introductory Session Worksheet

COPYING TEXT OF THE OLD TESTAMENT

If the only copy of the Scriptures you possessed was to be one you made for yourself, how would you do as a scribe? This activity is for use in the group session following Unit 1. Please follow carefully the instructions in completing the work.

Instructions:

Copy the scriptural text appearing below onto a sheet of paper using an ink pen. The following conditions will guide you as you work.

1. You have 10 minutes to copy as much of the text as you can.
2. You must print your work. You can make only one copy. If you make a mistake you cannot start over.
3. After you have finished, lay your copy aside for 24 hours. Then, read it side-by-side with the original for mistakes. Mark your mistakes but do not correct them.
4. Bring your copy of Jeremiah 36:1-8 with you to the group session.

Jeremiah 36:1-8, NIV

[1]In the fourth year of Jehoiakim son of Josiah king of
Judah, this word came to Jeremiah from the LORD.
[2]"Take a scroll and write on it all the words I have spo-
ken to you concerning Israel, Judah and all the other
nations from the time I began speaking to you in the
reign of Josiah till now. [3]Perhaps when the people of
Judah hear about every disaster I plan to inflict on
them, each of them will turn from his wicked way; then
I will forgive their wickedness and their sin."

[4]So Jeremiah called Baruch son of Neriah, and while
Jeremiah dictated all the words the LORD had spoken to
him, Baruch wrote them on the scroll. [5]Then Jeremiah
told Baruch, "I am restricted; I cannot go to the LORD's
temple. [6]So you go to the house of the LORD on a day
of fasting and read to the people from the scroll the
words of the LORD that you wrote as I dictated. Read
them to all the people of Judah who come in from their
towns. [7]Perhaps they will bring their petition before the
LORD, and each will turn from his wicked ways, for the
anger and wrath pronounced against this people by the
LORD are great.

[8]Baruch son of Neriah did everything Jeremiah the
prophet told him to do; at the LORD's temple he read
the words of the LORD from the scroll.

When you have finished, read all of Jeremiah 36 in the translation of your choice. Then, respond to the questions below.

1. How do you think Baruch felt when the king cut into pieces and burned the scroll?

2. What problems do you think Baruch and others faced in making copies of God's Word?

3. How did completing this activity affect your appreciation for those who spent their lives copying the Scriptures?

4. How did completing this activity affect your gratitude for God preserving and passing His Word on to His people over these thousands of years?

5. If you had to make a choice would you keep or destroy the copy you made? Give the reason for your answer.

GROUP SESSION 1 God and His Revelation

SESSION GOALS

At the conclusion of this session members will be able to:

1. Explain the historical and geographical background of the Old Testament Scriptures.
2. Identify key locations and people groups in the Old Testament.
3. State and illustrate the basic principles for interpreting the Old Testament.

Before the Session

❑ 1. Study carefully unit 1 and complete all learning activities. Review the session goals.

❑ 2. Pray for God's guidance as you prepare for this session. Pray specifically for each member of your group.

❑ 3. Read through "During the Session." Decide on the amount of time to allow for each segment of the Bible study. Write in the margin of your leader guide the time you want each segment to begin.

❑ 4. Gather the following materials:

- set of maps to use in the Bible study segment each week
- note paper
- yardstick

❑ 5. Extra Preparation:

- You may want to do additional reading related to the areas of Palestinian geography and the Old Testament Scriptures.
- Use a state map, a road atlas, or an encyclopedia to find the size of your state in square miles. Divide that by the number 10,000 to determine the size of Palestine in relation to your state. You will want to be prepared to share this in the group session.
- Contact your hosts if you are meeting in a home. Make certain they know when to expect the group and how many to prepare for.
- Provide for refreshments if they are being served during the break.
- Prepare a copy of the unit review quiz for each member.

During the Session

Part I
OPENING ACTIVITIES—25 MINUTES

1. Welcome members and begin with prayer. (5 mins.)
2. Memory Review: Have members pair off and quote the memory verses. Participate in this activity with the group. Pair yourself off with a different member each week. (5 mins.)
3. Distribute and have members complete the unit review quiz. When they have finished, lead a discussion of their answers. Be certain everyone has the correct answers. (10 mins.) Quiz Answers: 1-c; 2-a; 3-f; 4-b; 5-g; 6-d; 7-m; 8-e; 9-l;10-h; 11-k; 12-i; 13-j.

4. Sign Covenants: Go over the group covenant with the members. Allow them to ask questions, if there are any. Have members pass their books so everyone can sign each other's covenant. (5 mins.)

Part II
BIBLE STUDY AND GROUP DISCUSSION—50 MINUTES

Tell the group it is time to begin Bible study and group discussion of the material they studied during the previous week. You will want to select key questions from the following material to address in the group session.

The People and Geography of Palestine

Give members a minute to look at the matching activity (member book, p. 10) listing the many people groups in Palestine. Then have them open their books to the area map inside the front cover. Call out the names of the people groups and geographic regions in random order. Ask the group members to explain who the groups were and where they lived without looking at their materials.

Lead the group to discuss why the location of Palestine is significant. Start by asking, Why is the location of such a geographic area important? Ask members to recall the historic boundaries of Palestine (member book, p. 11).

Discuss matters related to the location of the Holy Land. Consider the following questions.

a. Why did those boundaries develop as they did?

b. Why do you think God placed His people in the natural land bridge we call Palestine?

Note that Palestine is a small area of land. Discuss the distances in miles covered in the area. Lead members to relate those distances to the place where they live. Draw parallels to be sure members grasp this. Examples may be taken from the distances to your state capital, or major cities near your location. Relate the relative size of Palestine to that of your state. For example, Palestine would fit about 4½ times in the state of Mississippi.

Say, "Keeping in mind the small size and population of Palestine, we know God has used it significantly in world events." Then ask, "What does this imply for our church?"

Have members recall the natural divisions of the land of Palestine (member book, pp. 13-14).

Have members recall the various names for the Sea of Galilee. Ask why this phenomenon occurs. Lead members to see that as populations live and die, sometimes the names of places change. If possible, relate this to a local setting (leader guide, p.16).

Have members recall the names of the rivers feeding into the East side of the Jordan River *(North to South: Yarmuk, Jabbok, Arnon, Zered, and the five regions formed by the streams Bashan, Gilead, Ammon, Moab, and Edom).*

Using the modern-day map, have members pinpoint the major geographic areas discussed in days 1 through 3.

The Old Testament Literature

Have members recall the divisions of the Old Testament literature *(Law, History, Poetry/Wisdom, Major Prophets, Minor Prophets).*

Next, have members recall the books within each division:

- The Books of the Law *(Genesis, Exodus, Leviticus, Numbers, Deuteronomy).*
- The Books of History *(Joshua, Judges, Ruth, 1 and 2 Samuel, 1 and 2 Kings, 1 and 2 Chronicles, Ezra, Nehemiah, Esther).*
- The Books of Poetry *(Job, Psalms, Proverbs, Ecclesiastes, Song of Solomon, Lamentations).*
- The Major Prophets *(Isaiah, Jeremiah, Ezekiel, Daniel).*
- The Minor Prophets *(Hosea, Joel, Amos, Obadiah, Jonah, Micah, Nahum, Habakkuk, Zephaniah, Haggai, Zechariah, Malachi).*

Show members the yardstick. Ask them to discuss how it is a standard of measurement. Have them recall things measured by inches, feet, or yards. Use this to introduce the discussion of the Canon of the Old Testament. Make sure everyone understands the concept of "canon." Lead members to express how the "canon" is our standard for ethical, moral, and religious conduct.

Have members recall the three parts of the Hebrew Bible *(Torah, Prophets, and Writings)*. Be sure they see the difference between the Hebrew and Christian Bibles.

Activity: Have members exchange their copies of the passage from the Book of Jeremiah, chapter 36. Ask them to check each other's manuscript against the copy of the original. Discuss the transmission of the Old Testament text and the difficulty the early copyists encountered. Ask, "How did this process increase their appreciation of the Scriptures?" (allow 10 mins.)

Ask members to recall the date of the oldest *complete* manuscript of the Old Testament *(A.D. 1008)*. Discuss the significance of the Dead Sea Scrolls (member book, p. 21). Remind members that God used human instruments to reveal His word to us *(example, Baruch)*. Ask, "What does this imply for us?"

Activity: Recall from memory the five principles of interpretation. Then give instructions for the following activity.

1. Assign numbers to the group members—1, 2, 3, 4, and 5.

2. Ask members to pair off by numbers. Each pair will look at and discuss the principle corresponding to their number. They will report to the group why that principle is important and what statement in *Step by Step Through the Old Testament* clarified that principle for them.

3. As time permits, refer to the Scripture passages and lead members in a discussion of the principles of interpretation using the author's illustrations. You want them to discuss and understand the five principles of interpretation. (These principles will appear in each of the odd numbered weekly review quizzes. Reinforce the use of these until the group develops the ability to think through the interpretative process on their own. It will help you as the group leader to go ahead and memorize them.)

CONCLUSION—10 MINUTES

1. Preview next week's materials. Ask members to look at the unit 2 overview. They will be studying the Creation, the Fall, Cain and Abel, the Flood, and the Tower of Babel. Assign a member to each area. The assigned member will need to prepare a two-minute summary of his topic for the next group session.

2. Remind members of the importance of doing the work. Encourage them to make time daily to work in their member books. They want to develop the practice of spending time with God daily. Encourage them to learn the memory verses. The memory verses will help them recall the significant themes in each unit.

After the Session

1. Carefully evaluate the effectiveness of the session. Use the questions that appear on page 11 in the course administrative plan to guide your evaluation.

2. Save any materials you have developed for use in future groups of *Step by Step Through the Old Testament*.

3. Immediately begin your preparations for next week's session. Make certain you have learned the memory verses.

4. Pray for the group. This week pray that your group members will hear God speak through the pages of the Old Testament.

GROUP SESSION 2 God and His Creation

SESSION GOALS

At the conclusion of this session members will:

1. Have an overview of the content of Genesis 1—11.

2. Be able to draw parallels between their lives and those of the people and circumstances in Genesis 1—11.

Before the Session

❑ 1. Study carefully unit 2 and complete all learning activities. Review the session goals above.

❑ 2. Pray for God's guidance as you prepare for this session. Pray specifically for each member of your group.

❑ 3. Read through "During the Session." Decide on the amount of time to allow for each segment of the Bible study. Write in the margin of your leader guide the time you want each segment to begin.

❑ 4. Prepare a copy of the unit review quiz for each member.

❑ 5. Prepare a two-minute summary of the next unit to share in the assignments section.

During the Session

Part I
OPENING ACTIVITIES—20 MINUTES

1. Welcome members and begin with prayer. (5 mins.)

2. Memory Review: Have members pair off and quote the memory verses. Participate in this activity with the group. Pair yourself off with a different member each week. (5 mins.)

3. Distribute and have members complete the unit review quiz. When they have finished, lead a discussion of their answers. Be certain everyone has the correct answers. (10 mins.) Quiz Answers: 1-c; 2-g; 3-f; 4-d; 5-i; 6-j; 7-a; 8-h; 9-b; 10-e.

Part II
BIBLE STUDY AND GROUP DISCUSSION—50 MINUTES

A General Discussion of Genesis
Engage members in a discussion of some general background about the Book of Genesis. Make certain they understand the following:

- The two periods of Old Testament history covered in Genesis.

- The role of Genesis in the materials we call the Pentateuch.

- The difference in the two accounts of the creation.

- The general outline or progression of thought in the text *(Creation, Fall, Tower of Babel, and Flood).*

God and Creation: Genesis 1:1—2:3)
Ask members to discuss the significance of the use of *bara* in Genesis 1. Use the following questions to lead a discussion of the creation of humankind.

- What is the significance of *bara* being used only of God?

- If humanity is the supreme work of God in creation, what does that say about the value of human life?

In the Image of God
Ask members what it means to be "in the image of God" (1:27). What does the idea that both male and female are in God's image mean to you? (member book, p. 28).

Read the author's statement, "To 'rule over' (1:26) means to use the creation for the common good of humanity and according to God's purposes" (member book, p. 28). Ask members to discuss:

- What are some abuses of humanity's ability to "rule over"?

- What are some ways Christians can set a positive example in ruling over the earth?

Making Choices: Genesis 3:1-7
Ask a member to state a general summary of what happened in the garden with the serpent, the woman, and the man.

Ask a member to explain why we call the temptation and failure of Adam and Eve "the fall" (member book, p. 32).

Discuss the significance of the trees. Ask what the trees represent (choice, [member book, p. 31]). Stimulate a discussion of some "trees" that are part of our lives.

Examples:
1. Selfishness—surrender to Christ.
2. Service—lack of commitment.
3. Moral purity—immorality.

Make reference to the author's statement "He [the serpent] started Adam and Eve thinking that God chose to deprive them of something that would be good for them" (member book, p. 32). Ask members to state some ways this form of thinking is evident in our world today.

Accepting Consequences: Genesis 3:8-23
Read the statement on page 32 of the member book, "their sin was ... rebellion against God and rejection of His commands." Note that this self-ruled life is the essence of sin.

Next, read the statement "Each sin brings its own consequences." Ask members to name some ways we see this in the world around us (member book, p. 34).

The following event happened in a church I pastored during seminary. As you tell the story, have members listen for parallels to how the story illustrates the nature of sin.

A particular child was exposed to chicken pox in the daycare center she attended each day in New Orleans. The following weekend, she went to church and subsequently exposed the children in the church nursery. Those children then went home and exposed their older siblings. From the church nursery chicken pox entered the local school system.

Use the following questions to help generate discussion.

- Ask members to make observations about how the story illustrates the nature of sin.

- Ask the members to offer from their observation other physical examples of how sin spreads. Lead them to see that our sin always affects others.

The Significance of the Punishments:
Activity: Divide the group into three subgroups and give the following assignments.

a. Group 1: Discuss and report on the most significant aspect of the serpent's punishment.

b. Group 2: Discuss and report on the most significant aspect of the woman's punishment.

c. Group 3: Discuss and report on the most significant aspect of the man's punishment.

Allow five minutes for discussion. Call the groups back to the large group and ask for reports.

When finished, ask, "What was the most significant aspect of the humans' punishment?" *(Alienation between God and between themselves)*

Cain and Abel: Genesis 4
Have a member summarize the events related to Cain and Abel.

Ask the members to tell their response to why they think God accepted one offering but rejected the other (member book, p. 36).

Lead members to see that even in punishment, God provided for Cain's protection.

The Flood: Genesis 6
Have the assigned member give his summary of the events leading up to and occurring during the flood.

Have members turn in their books to page 38. Ask them to read again Genesis 6:5-9 and then share their responses to the four questions about how sin affects God.

The Tower of Babel
Have the member assigned give his summary of the events of the Tower of Babel.

Ask the group to name ways the sin of Genesis 11 was similar and dissimilar to that of Adam and Eve.

Drawing Some Conclusions
Have members turn to page 40 in their books. Allow them to share the lessons that stand out to them related to the accounts of the creation, fall, flood, and tower of Babel.

CONCLUSION—10 MINUTES

1. Use the two-minute summary you prepared to preview next week's materials. Refer members to the unit learning goals.

2. Pray together. Allow members to share requests.

After the Session

1. Carefully evaluate the effectiveness of the session. Use the questions that appear on page 14 in the course administrative plan to guide your evaluation.

2. Save any materials you have developed for use in future groups of *Step by Step Through the Old Testament*.

3. Immediately begin your preparations for next week's session. Make certain you have learned the memory verses.

4. Pray for the group. This week pray for their openness to hear God speak to them in the call of Abraham.

GROUP SESSION 3 *God and the Patriarchs*

SESSION GOALS

At the conclusion of this session members will:

1. Be able to state how God worked in the lives of the Patriarchs.
2. Understand the Old Testament concept of Covenant.
3. Be able to state lessons from the lives of the Patriarchs.

Before the Session

- ❑ 1. Study carefully unit 3 and complete all learning activities. Review the session goals.
- ❑ 2. Pray for God's guidance as you prepare for this session. Pray specifically for each member of your group.
- ❑ 3. Read through "During the Session." Decide on the amount of time to allow for each segment of the Bible study. Write in the margin of your leader guide the time you want each segment to begin.
- ❑ 4. Prepare a copy of the unit review quiz for each member and gather other materials as needed.
- ❑ 5. Look up the meaning of the word *patriarch* in a good dictionary. Be prepared to share the meaning with the group.

During the Session

Part I
OPENING ACTIVITIES—20 MINUTES

1. Welcome members and begin with prayer. (5 mins.)
2. Memory Review: Have members pair off and quote the memory verses. Participate in this activity with the group. Pair yourself off with a different member each week. (5 mins.)
3. Distribute and have members complete the unit review quiz. When they have finished, lead a discussion of their answers. Be certain everyone has the correct answers. (10 mins.) Quiz Answers: 1-e; 2-f; 3-d; 4-i; 5-c; 6-j; 7-b; 8-h; 9-a; 10-g.

Part II
BIBLE STUDY AND GROUP DISCUSSION—50 MINUTES

The Patriarchs and the Call of Abraham (Gen. 12:1-5)
Ask the members to recall the names of the four Patriarchs (Abraham, Isaac, Jacob, Joseph). Ask a member to recall the meaning of the word *patriarch*. If no one knows, share the meaning of the term with them.

Make reference to the author's statement "God chose Abraham and his descendants to carry out His work in the world" (member book, p. 41). Without using the term *witness*, ask members to discuss how God can use people today. (You want them to express the idea in non-religious terms.)

Map Check: Have a member pinpoint on the map the areas relative to this session's content (Ur, the Tigris and Euphrates Rivers, the "fertile crescent," Haran, Schechem, Bethel, Canaan, the Negev Desert).

Remind the members that the journey Abraham and his family took was around 1500 miles. Ask them to share their ideas of the type fears and difficulties such travel entailed (member book, p. 42).

Ask members to share how they think God called Abraham. Was it by an audible voice or an inner conviction? Ask them why they feel that way (member book, p. 43).

Ask members to discuss this question: How does God lead us? Help them see He leads us through the work of the Holy Spirit as we pray, study the Word, evaluate circumstances, and hear the encouragement of the church.

Blessings and Difficulties

Ask members to state some of the blessings and difficulties they see as a result of following God.

Refer the group to the activity on page 43 of the member book. Review the activity to make sure members understand the promises God gave to Abraham.

Ask members to share struggles they may have had with the call of God. Abraham obeyed God. Help them see knowing the will of God begins with an obedient, faith relationship with God.

Say, Faith means trusting God and doing what He leads you to do. Make this statement. In the Bible, faith does not exist apart from action. Ask members to think of other biblical examples, and what they think this implies for our lives.

Refer members to the list of responses to difficulties and hardships found on page 45 of the member book. Ask them to discuss the ones with which they identify.

Abraham and Lot (Genesis 13—14)

Ask a member to summarize the events leading up to Lot moving to Sodom and Gomorrah.

Make this statement, Sometimes material blessings create problems in human relationships. Then ask, "How is this true or untrue?"

Mention that Lot chose that area for its prosperity. Ask, "What are some dangers of allowing the promise of prosperity to dictate our choices?"

Have members look at the agree/disagree statements appearing on page 46 of the member book. After they read over them, ask them to agree or disagree with the statements. In the discussion, you want them to tell why they feel a certain way. Have them give biblical reasons for their convictions. Ask them what they think Lot's answers would have been before, and after, the disaster of Sodom and Gomorrah.

God's Covenant with Abraham (Gen. 15—17)

Have members recall the five characteristics of God's covenant with Abraham.

Read Genesis 15:1-5. Ask members to discuss how God responded to being questioned. Note that Abraham questioned God (Gen. 15:2,8). Then ask members to respond to the following questions.

- Have you heard it said that "We are not supposed to question God"?
- How do you feel about Abram questioning God?
- How do you feel about God's response?
- What is the lesson for us? Notice Abraham questioned God the second time *after* he had believed.

Abraham and Hagar (Gen. 16)

Refer members to the first paragraph under this heading in their books on page 46. Help them understand that these events took place hundreds of years before the Law was received on Mt. Sinai. The arrangement with Hagar was acceptable in that day. Ask members if there are similar practices happening today. (For example, surrogate parenthood is not too far removed from Abraham's arrangement.)

Note that doing things our way instead of God's is always a sign of unbelief. Abraham and Sarah apparently acted because they did not believe God (member book, p. 46).

Have members scan over their responses to "Responding to God's Word" on page 47 in their books. Ask them to share why it seems so hard to wait on God's timing.

Abraham and Isaac

Note for the members that in the birth of Isaac, God fulfilled His promise to provide Abraham an heir. From here, lead members to discuss the activity on page 49 in their member book concerning Abraham's response to God's command to sacrifice Isaac.

Refer to the lessons the author offers on page 48 of the member book. The primary lesson in the Isaac story is that God wants us to yield ourselves totally to Him, becoming "living sacrifices" in our service for Christ.

Remind members that after a time, Abraham sent a servant to find a wife for Isaac. The servant prayed for God's guidance (Gen. 24:10-26). Ask members to share how God has given them guidance in specific situations.

Isaac, Esau, and Jacob

Refer members to the activity on page 51, concerning the moral correctness of Jacob's treatment of Esau. Ask the group to decide whether they consider Jacob's actions right or wrong.

Read the statement appearing on page 52, "In ancient times people believed spoken words could never be retracted. In reality, this is still true. You may ask forgiveness for your words, you may confess your wrong speech, but words can't be taken back."

Have members recall an experience in their own lives in which someone's words caused them great joy or pain, or greatly encouraged or discouraged them. Allow several to share as they feel comfortable.

Ask members to discuss how it makes them feel to know that God can use imperfect instruments (like Jacob and us) to accomplish His perfect work.

Refer members to Jacob's dream in Genesis 28:10-22. Note that in that experience Jacob had his first real experience with God. Next, refer members to Genesis 32. Briefly summarize for them the events leading up to Jacob's reunion with Esau. Note for them that in this encounter God changed Jacob's life and made him His person. Refer members to the four ways Jacob responded to God (p. 54). Ask members to share promises God has made to them in His Word, and the experiences that confirmed the truth of God's promise.

Jacob and Joseph

Have a member summarize briefly Joseph's story. Ask, "How many of you have (or did have) siblings? If you had to identify yourself, would you identify more with Joseph or his brothers?" Ask members to think of ways they can relate to Joseph.

Ask members to share why they think God preserved and blessed Joseph's life.

Ask, "What Christlike characteristics do you find in Joseph's life?"

Refer members to "Responding to God's Word" on page 56. Ask if there are any lessons in the lives of the Patriarchs they want to share with the group.

CONCLUSION—10 MINUTES

1. Preview next week's materials. Tell members that this coming week they will begin their study of the events surrounding the Exodus.

2. Make this assignment: Ask group members to go (as individuals) to a nearby lake or other large body of water during the week. As they sit on the bank, ask them to meditate on these questions: How would I cross this if someone chasing me planned to kill me? What fears would go through my mind?

After the Session

1. Carefully evaluate the effectiveness of the session. Use the questions that appear on page 14 in the course administrative plan to guide your evaluation.

2. Save any materials you have developed for use in future groups of *Step by Step Through the Old Testament*.

3. Immediately begin your preparations for next week's session. Make certain you have learned the memory verses.

4. This week pray for members' vision of how God acts on our behalf to declare His power and glory.

GROUP SESSION 4 God and the Exodus

SESSION GOALS

At the conclusion of this session members will:

1. Understand that God's presence with us enables us to face all of life's circumstances.
2. Be able to identify ways we run ahead of God.
3. Be able to identify ways God uses the circumstances of life to prepare us for His service.

Before the Session

❑ 1. Study carefully unit 4 and complete all learning activities. Review the session goals.

❑ 2. Pray for God's guidance as you prepare for this session. Pray specifically for each member of your group.

❑ 3. Read through "During the Session." Decide on the amount of time to allow for each segment of the Bible study. Look ahead and see where the follow-up on last week's identification assignment appears in the session. Write in the margin of your leader guide the time you want each segment to begin.

❑ 4. Prepare a copy of the unit review quiz for each member and gather other materials as needed.

❑ 5. By now the group is in a routine. Think about where you will sit for this session. Plan to change your seat at session 8. Observe how this move effects the group dynamics.

During the Session

Part I
OPENING ACTIVITIES—20 MINUTES

1. Welcome members and begin with prayer. (5 mins.)
2. Memory Review: Have members pair off and quote the memory verses. Participate in this activity with the group. Pair yourself off with a different member each week. (5 mins.)
3. Distribute and have members complete the unit review quiz. When all have finished, discuss the quiz making certain everyone has the correct answers. (10 mins.) Quiz Answers: 1-b; 2-i; 3-f; 4-e; 5-a; 6-d; 7-h; 8-j; 9-g; 10-c.

Part II
BIBLE STUDY AND GROUP DISCUSSION—50 MINUTES

Have group members open their Bibles to the Book of Exodus as you begin this session.

Israel in Egypt (Ex. 1)
State that in the Book of Exodus, we have the Ten Commandments, the making of the covenant, the crossing of the sea, the tabernacle, and other important teachings.

Ask a member to summarize the events leading to the enslavement of the Hebrews in Egypt.

The Birth of Moses (Ex. 2:1-10)
Have a member summarize the events surrounding the birth of Moses.

Ask, "Why do you think many historical details are not included in the biblical record of Moses' birth?" Allow several members to respond (p. 59).

Have members recall the three types of oppression the Hebrew people suffered in Egypt. *(oppression by forced labor, infanticide, murder of the male children)* Then ask them to respond to these questions:

- Have you ever been treated unjustly?
- How did you respond?
- What happened to relieve it?

Ask the members to answer the following questions:

- Are you aware of sacrifice made by people you know who helped you come to Christ?
- What sacrifice did significant people in your life make for you to know Christ? ("Responding to God's Word," p. 60)

Moses (Ex. 2:11—3:5)

Remind members that Moses was reared in the palace of the Pharaoh and had the finest his day could offer in privilege, education, and comfort. However, he identified with his people.

Refer members to Exodus 2:12. Moses "killed the Egyptian and hid him in the sand." Read the author's statement, "However, Moses ran ahead of God's plan." Then ask the group to discuss ways we run ahead of God (member book, p. 60).

Refer members to the author's statement that "Even in Midian God worked to prepare Moses for what he would do later" (member book, p.61). Ask members to share how God has used things in their lives to prepare them for later service.

The Call of Moses (Ex. 2:23—6:1)

Briefly summarize the events surrounding Moses' call. Then state that because God spoke to Moses at Mt. Horeb, it became identified with the presence of God.

Ask members to share their answers to the following questions.

- Can you recall an event in your life that would be your Mt. Horeb?
- What are some ways God has spoken to you in the ordinary affairs of life? (member book, p. 62)

State that Moses stood on holy ground at Mt. Horeb. In the ancient world, taking the shoes off indicated reverence. Taking his shoes off his feet (Ex. 3:5) showed the reverence Moses had for God. Ask, "In present-day terms, what is holy ground? How do we show reverence for God?"

Moses' Call and Excuses (Ex. 3:6—9:35)

Ask members to recall the five excuses Moses offered *(not worthy, don't know enough about God, people will not believe me, cannot speak in public, send somebody else)* (member book, p. 63).

Ask members to share which of Moses' excuses they have used, and how God responded to them (member book, p. 63).

Ask members to discuss the significance of God's response to Moses in Exodus 3:11-12, "I will be with you." Ask, "How would this assurance help us face any task God has for us?"

Read the statement that appears on page 65 in the member book, "All of these signs had a purpose. God gave them so the people might believe Moses' message that the Lord God of Abraham, the God of Isaac, and the God of Jacob had appeared to Moses. The signs would validate his message from God." Then ask members to discuss this statement: "God always manifests His power to reveal Himself and bring others to Him; never to glorify men or exalt to status of a particular church." Ask members to identify and discuss ways we can be guilty of coveting (or stealing) God's glory.

Ask volunteers to share evidences from their own experience or observation that God equips people to do what He leads them to do.

Have members recall the list of plagues (member book, p. 69). Note that the plagues were the response of God to the hardness of Pharaoh's heart. Refer to the author's statement that the idea of Pharaoh's heart being hardened "probably means God allowed Pharaoh to have his own way" (member book, p. 67).

Next, ask members to share their responses to "Responding to God's Word" on page 68 related to hardening one's heart and choosing one's own way. Use these questions to encourage discussion.

- Can you recall a point in your life when you willfully chose to go your own way instead of God's way?

- What are some of the negative things that happen when we harden our hearts to God's will?

- Share times when you know you chose your own way over God's and the result.

- What did God teach you in the experience?

Ask members to recall the two purposes of the plagues *(they showed the people of Israel and the people of Egypt that the Lord is God, and the plagues assured the release of the Hebrews)* (member book, p. 68).

Engage the group in a discussion of how these two purposes challenged the popular views of the Egyptians *(Pharaoh's child died, the Nile was filled with death, the sun was darkened, and the animals died)*.

The Crossing of the Red Sea (Ex. 13:17—14:31)
Have a member briefly summarize the events of the Red Sea crossing.

Activity: Allow members to respond to the activity they were assigned last week. Encourage members to share insight they have gained about the power of God in this activity. The following questions will help.

- Did you choose a body of water or a locked room for the exercise?

- How did it make you feel to think that you were trapped with someone who was about to kill you?

- How do you think the Hebrews felt when facing the sea with the attacking Egyptians behind them?

As time permits, allow group members to discuss the "Responding to God's Word" activity on page 71 in their member books.

CONCLUSION—10 MINUTES

1. Use the two-minute summary you prepared to preview next week's materials. Make the following assignment:

   Ask members to review some type of covenant document. It can be a copy of the Church Covenant, a financial contract, or some other type document they possess. They will want to read it with a view to seeing the conditions, privileges, and commitments of that covenant. Tell them to bring a copy of the document with them to the next session.

2. Allow members to share prayer concerns, then pray together for those matters.

After the Session

1. Carefully evaluate the effectiveness of the session. Use the questions that appear on page 14 in the course administrative plan to guide your evaluation.

2. Save any materials you have developed for use in future groups of *Step by Step Through the Old Testament*.

3. Immediately begin your preparations for next week's session. Make certain you have learned the memory verses.

4. Pray for the group. This week pray for their understanding of God's covenant love for His people.

GROUP SESSION 5 God and His Law

SESSION GOALS

At the conclusion of this session members will:

1. Understand the conditions of the Sinai covenant.
2. Be able to state the three promises of the covenant.
3. Be able to make contemporary applications of the Ten Commandments.

Before the Session

- ❑ 1. Study carefully unit 5 and complete all learning activities. Review the group session goals.
- ❑ 2. Pray for God's guidance as you prepare for this session. Pray specifically for each member of your group.
- ❑ 3. Read through "During the Session." Decide on the amount of time to allow for each segment of the Bible study. Make certain you note where the follow-up on last week's identification assignment is located. Write in the margin of your leader guide the time you want each segment to begin.
- ❑ 4. Prepare a copy of the unit review quiz for each member. Gather other materials as needed.
- ❑ 5. Prepare a two-minute overview of the next unit to share with the members.

During the Session

Part I
OPENING ACTIVITIES—20 MINUTES

1. Welcome members and begin with prayer. (5 mins.)
2. Memory Review: Have members pair off and quote the memory verses. Participate in this activity with the group. Pair yourself off with a different member each week. (5 mins.)
3. Distribute and have members complete the unit review quiz. When they have finished, lead a discussion of their answers. Be certain everyone has the correct answers. (10 mins.) Quiz Answers: 1-h; 2-e; 3-f; 4-d; 5-g; 6-c; 7-i; 8-b; 9-j; 10-a.

Part II
BIBLE STUDY AND GROUP DISCUSSION—50 MINUTES

Have the group members open their Bibles to Exodus 19 as you begin this session.

An Introduction to the Covenant with the Nation (Ex. 19:3-7)
Ask members to recall the basic purposes of the Books of Leviticus and Numbers given on page 72 of the member book.

Use the following questions to lead a discussion of the covenant.

- What were the two conditions of the covenant? *(obey God fully, keep His covenant)*
- What were the three terms or promises of the covenant? *(treasured possession, kingdom of priests, holy nation)*

Ask a member to recall the author's definition of covenant *(the establishing of a relationship)*. Make reference to Jeremiah 31:31-33 and be certain members understand how that definition applies.

Ask members to recall the three essential elements of the Sinai covenant.

- First, God based His covenant on His acts in history.
- Second, God gave conditions for the covenant.
- Third, the covenant contains the promises of God. (The promises were previously mentioned.) Lead members to discuss the significance of being God's treasured possession, a kingdom of priests and a holy nation.

Activity: Have members discuss the covenants they examined during the week. As they tell briefly about the covenants, have them state the conditions, privileges, and penalties specified in the particular documents. You want them to see the covenant concept is still in use.

The Ten Commandments (Ex. 20)

Move into a discussion of the commandments. Help members see that even if the literary divisions are different, the spirit of the law remains unchanged. No matter how they are divided, the commandments are basic to the moral fiber of Christianity.

Help the members see the form of the commandments (member book, p. 76). Ask them to identify the commandments that pertain to our relationship to God *(commandments 1-4)* and the ones that pertain to our relationship with other people *(commandments 6-10)*.

Ask members to share insights gained as they looked at the commandments.

Refer to the activity on page 77 of the member book (Commandment 1), and have members help you identify other religions represented in your community or area. Ask, "How should Christians relate to people who worship other gods?"

The Commandments and Our Relationship to God

Have members open their Bibles to Exodus 20:1-11. As time permits, you may do all of these, or you may choose certain commandments. As you read the commandments, engage members in a discussion. Ask the suggested questions (and others you may think of) that will clarify ways we both keep and break the commandments. Help members see our goal is to faithfully obey all the commandments of God.

First—"You shall have no other gods before me." Ask, "Is it possible to have other 'gods' in the place of the Lord God? If so, how?"

Second—"You shall not make for yourself any idol in the form of anything in heaven above or on the earth beneath or in the waters below." Ask, "How many of you have any type of visual representation of Jesus in your homes or churches?" Then ask members to respond to the following questions.

- How do such objects reflect our "image" or perception of God?
- Do such icons depict Jesus as clean or dirty, handsome or homely? Is the picture racially identifiable?
- Should we allow the placement of such objects in our homes or churches? Why or why not?

Have members list the following items in the margin of their member's book: eating, bathing, work, family, leisure, time with God. Then have them number from one to six (one being most important, six being least important) in order of the current priority they are giving them. When they have finished, ask, "What did you learn about yourself and your worship of God?" The purpose of this activity is to help the group members evaluate their personal worship habits.

Third—"You shall not misuse the name of the Lord your God." Ask members to elaborate on what it means to take God's name and character lightly. Help them see this goes far deeper than simple vocabulary. At its root such "profanity" is an attitude of life. Thus, it is entirely possible for one's whole life, family, or even a church, to be a profanity before God.

Fourth—"Remember the Sabbath day by keeping it holy." Remind members that we worship on the Lord's day (Sunday) as opposed to the Jewish sabbath (Saturday). Ask members to respond to these questions:

- Should we develop an elaborate system of do's and don'ts regarding the "Sabbath Day?"

- What is the line between legalistic ritual and real worship? *(It is when we move our security onto a foundation of tradition and legalism as opposed to a vital relationship with God.)*

Note the response activity on page 78 "Responding to God's Word." "Not all Christians agree on how to observe the Lord's Day." Have the members share some of the ways they listed that Christians can please and honor the Lord on the Lord's Day.

The Commandments and Our Relationship to Others
Fifth—"Honor your father and your mother." Note that "when we rightly worship God, we show true care for our earthly parents." The commandments were given to the nation, and to individuals only as part of the nation. Have members discuss whether they agree or disagree with the author's statement "a society without concern for human beings cannot endure."

Sixth—"You shall not murder." Have several members share their insights regarding this commandment based on Matthew 5:21-26.

Seventh—"You shall not commit adultery." This area may be sensitive. Address it by having members discuss the seven true/false statements appearing on page 80 of the member book.

Eighth—"You shall not steal." Have members deal with the eighth commandment by discussing their responses to the agree/disagree statements on page 80 of the member book.

Ninth—"You shall not give false testimony." Read the author's statement, "apart from honesty and integrity, justice cannot prevail" (member book, p. 80). Note that in ancient Israel the loss of reputation could mean the loss of business, family, even life. Ask how this is true today.

Ask members to read Ruth 4:9-11 and discuss why such transactions took place in the city gates. *(It was public, there were plenty of witnesses, the elders heard the case.)* Ask them what forum we have for this process today. *(the church, and in most places, the court system)*

Tenth—"You shall not covet." Help members to see the contemporary applications of coveting. Note that if this commandment is obeyed, the other commandments will not be as difficult to obey.

The Book of the Covenant (Ex. 20:22—23:33)
Note this name is taken from Exodus 24:7. State that the book of the covenant is an application of the Ten Commandments to particular cases.

Activity: Divide your group into pairs. Assign one of the principles reflected in the book of the covenants to each pair (member book, p. 81). Ask them to state the principle, and at least one illustration of the principle. Allow five minutes to work, then call for reports.

The Tabernacle (Ex. 25—31; 35—40)
Remind members that the tabernacle symbolized God dwelling with His people (member book, pp. 82-83). Ask members to state the significance of the individual furnishings in the tabernacle. Note the ark of the covenant symbolized God's presence with His people (25:17).

- Table of the bread of the Presence: Reminded the people that God gave them the necessities of life (25:23-30).

- The lampstand: Reminded the people the way to God always is lighted (27:31-40).

- The altar of incense: Indicated prayer, and God's eternal presence with the people (30:1-10).

- The bronze basin: Signified the need for purity on the part of the person coming to meet God (30:17-21).

- The altar for burned offerings: Addressed the people's need for forgiveness (27:1-8).

Ask members to identify furnishings in your worship center that are paralleled in Exodus 25—31.

Allow members to share what they think is the most significant message the chapters about the Tabernacle hold for us today.

The Breaking and Renewal of the Covenant (Ex. 32—34)

Use the true/false statements on page 84 of the member book to cover the events of Sinai in which the people broke the covenant.

Read Exodus 34:6. Ask members how they feel in knowing God forgave even Israel.

The Book of Leviticus

State the following basic facts about Leviticus:

- It showed how sinful people were to come into the presence of God.

- It gave specific directions for the conduct of sacrifice before God.

Note that chapter 16 is the central chapter of the Book. Chapter 16 addresses the Day of Atonement. The rituals in the Day of Atonement were the ways the entire nation went before God in confession and seeking forgiveness.

The Book of Numbers

Ask a member to recall the primary focus of Numbers *(to record the wilderness experiences of the people)*.

Refer the group to the account of the spies in Numbers 13:1-3,26-33; 14:1-9. Then read Hebrews 3:16-18. Ask members to discuss their responses to the following questions.

- What is the relationship between disobedience (sin) and unbelief? *(It is the same thing.)*

- What does that have to say to us?

CONCLUSION—10 MINUTES

1. Use the two-minute summary you prepared to preview next week's materials. Refer members to the unit learning goals.

2. Optional. Make the following assignment: The members are to think about the most significant blessing of God on their lives. They are then to draw, mold from modeling clay, or fashion from some other material an object that would symbolize that blessing. If they wish, they may choose some item they already have in their home. They are to bring the object to the next group session.

3. Ask members to share prayer concerns and pray together.

After the Session

1. Carefully evaluate the effectiveness of the session. Use the questions that appear on page 14 in the course administrative plan to guide your evaluation.

2. Save any materials you have developed for use in future groups of *Step by Step Through the Old Testament.*

3. Immediately begin your preparations for next week's session. Make certain you have learned the memory verses.

4. Pray for the group. This week pray for their ability to obey God in every circumstance of life.

GROUP SESSION 6 God and the Land of Promise

SESSION GOALS

At the conclusion of this session members will be able to:

1. Recall and state the significance of the three major feasts.
2. Apply the *Shema* to their personal lives. *[Shema* refers to Deut. 6:4-9. The word comes from the first Hebrew word in the paragraph; the word means *hear.*]
3. Define and apply the concept of corporate sin and responsibility.

Before the Session

❑ 1. Study carefully unit 6 and complete all learning activities. Review the group session goals.

❑ 2. Pray for God's guidance as you prepare for this session. Pray specifically for each member of your group.

❑ 3. Read through "During the Session." Decide on the amount of time to allow for each segment of the Bible study. Make certain you note where the follow-up on last week's identification assignment is located. Write in the margin of your leader guide the time you want each segment to begin.

❑ 4. Prepare a copy of the unit review quiz for each member and gather other materials as needed.

❑ 5. Prepare a two-minute overview of the next unit to share with the members.

During the Session

Part I
OPENING ACTIVITIES—20 MINUTES

1. Welcome members and begin with prayer. (5 mins.)
2. Memory Review: Have members pair off and quote the memory verses. Participate in this activity with the group. Pair yourself off with a different member each week. (5 mins.)
3. Distribute and have members complete the unit review quiz. When they have finished, lead a discussion of their answers. Be certain everyone has the correct answers. (10 mins.) Quiz Answers: 1-j; 2-g; 3-d; 4-a; 5-c; 6-b; 7-e; 8-f; 9-h; 10-i.

Part II
BIBLE STUDY AND GROUP DISCUSSION—50 MINUTES

Have the group open their Bibles to the Book of Deuteronomy as you begin this session.

The Book of Deuteronomy—Moses' First Address (Deut. 1—4)
Have a member recall the Hebrew meaning of the title "Deuteronomy." *(these are the words)*

Ask members to recall the primary context of the Book of Deuteronomy. *(the words of Moses to the people while in Moab)*

Refer members to Deuteronomy 4:1-2. Ask members to discuss their responses to the following questions:

- How do we add to God's commandments today?

- How do we take away from God's commandments today?

Read Deuteronomy 6:4-9. Ask members to answer the following questions:

- What is the importance of faith and religious instruction in the home?
- Can you recall the names of significant religious leaders who were products of a strong Christian home?

Passing a Good Time (Deut. 8)
Refer members to Deuteronomy 8:1-20. Ask them to discuss why they think it is so easy to forget God when things are going well.

Ask members to name the three primary feasts of the Israelites *(Passover, Pentecost, Tabernacles)* and discuss what the feasts commemorated in Hebrew life.

Have members name the annual emphases or observances in the life of their church. Invite members to tell which of the annual emphases are most meaningful to them and why.

The Book of Joshua
Begin with the person to your right, and have the members name in order the Books of History *(Joshua, Judges, Ruth, 1 and 2 Samuel, 1 and 2 Kings, 1 and 2 Chronicles, Ezra, Nehemiah, Esther, Job).*

Use the following questions to introduce the Book of Joshua. (Some answers are at the beginning of day 3 and others are on the unit page.)

- What are the two parts of the Book of Joshua? *(the conquest and the division of the land)*
- Who is the author of Joshua? *(anonymous)*
- What is the primary message of Joshua? *(God's leadership of Israel as they took possession of the land He gave them)*

Using a map, have a member tell the sequence of the events in the period of the conquest.

Read Joshua 1:1-15. Ask members to share their response to God's commission to Joshua. You may refer back to the call of Moses to help them see the similarities in the promises. Ask members to share what it means to them personally.

Ask a member to recall the events surrounding the crossing of the Jordan River. How do you think the priests felt? What do you think the people were thinking? Why did the Lord have them get stones from the river bed after they had crossed the Jordan?

Activity: Have members show the object they brought that is symbolic of the significant blessing of God in their lives. Ask volunteers to show their object and tell about the blessing it symbolizes.

Using the map, make sure members see the divisions of the land. Share the following mnemonic (memory) device with them to help them learn the twelve tribes: S. J. BEDMIZAN, MGR. (Simeon, Judah, Benjamin, Ephraim, Dan, Manasseh, Issachar, Zebulun, Asher, Naphtali, Manasseh, Gad, Reuben). Original authorship unknown. I first heard this while a student at New Orleans Baptist Theological Seminary, in the introductory course to Old Testament under Waylon Bailey.

Sin and Corporate Responsibility (Josh. 7:10-12,19-23)
Note the author's statements on page 99, "Achan's sin resulted in God's removing His protection from the people of Israel." Have members share their definitions of corporate responsibility. When the concept has been clearly stated, lead the members in a discussion of corporate responsibility. Use the following questions to lead a discussion of corporate responsibility.

- What does it mean to be holy?
- How did Achan's sin affect others?
- What are some ways sin harms others besides the one doing the sinning?
- What are some implications of this for our families and our church?

The Book of Judges
Have a member tell the primary message of Judges *(it continues the history of God's people).*

Ask a member to recall the role of the judge in ancient Israel *(a deliverer, or a political/military leader who led the people during a time of hardship).*

Ask the group to recall the four stages in the cycle of Israel's life *(rebellion, oppression, repentance, deliverance).* Then ask volunteers to share ways they have seen this cycle in contemporary circumstances.

Ask members to recall what distinguishes a major judge from a minor judge *(the amount of biblical text given that particular judge).*

Ask the members to state lessons they may have drawn from the accounts of Deborah and Gideon. Ask, "What primary lesson do we draw from the life of Samson?" *(potential apart from responsibility and service is useless).*

As time allows, lead members to discuss the review section at the end of unit 6.

CONCLUSION—10 MINUTES

1. Use the two-minute summary you prepared to preview next week's materials. Refer members to the unit learning goals. There is no optional assignment this week.

2. Ask members to share prayer concerns and lead them to pray together.

After the Session

1. Carefully evaluate the effectiveness of the session. Use the questions that appear on page 14 in the course administrative plan to guide your evaluation.

2. Save any materials you have developed for use in future groups of *Step by Step Through the Old Testament.*

3. Immediately begin your preparation for next week's session. Make certain you have learned the memory verse.

4. Pray for the group. This week pray for their ability to look at people according to their inward self as opposed to their outward appearance.

GROUP SESSION 7 God and the Beginning of the Monarchy

SESSION GOALS

At the conclusion of this session members will be able to:

1. State three reasons King Saul failed in his leadership of Israel.

2. State a lesson each from the lives of Samuel, Saul, and David.

3. Be able to state differences in the relationship to God of Saul and David.

Before the Session

❑ 1. Study carefully unit 7 and complete all learning activities. Review the session goals.

❑ 2. Pray for God's guidance as you prepare for this session. Pray specifically for each member of your group.

❑ 3. Read through "During the Session." Decide on the amount of time to allow for each segment of the Bible study. Write in the margin of your leader guide the time you want each segment to begin.

❑ 4. Prepare a copy of the unit review quiz for each member and gather other materials as needed.

❑ 5. Prepare a two-minute overview of the next unit to share with the members.

❑ 6. Extra preparation: Before the session prepare to discuss or answer questions about the following subjects.
- Polygamy
- Saul's encounter with the witch of Endor
- The suicide of Saul
- Urim and Thummim.

During the Session

Part I
OPENING ACTIVITIES—20 MINUTES

1. Welcome members and begin with prayer. (5 mins).

2. Memory Review: Have members pair off and quote the memory verses. Participate in this activity with the group. Pair yourself off with a different member each week. (5 mins.)

3. Distribute and have members complete the unit review quiz. Then lead a discussion of their answers. (10 mins.) Answers: 1-e; 2-m; 3-f; 4-d; 5-l; 6-g; 7-c; 8-j; 9-h; 10-b; 11-k; 12-i; 13-a.

Part II
BIBLE STUDY AND GROUP DISCUSSION—50 MINUTES

God and the Beginning of the Monarchy
Ask a member to tell the meaning of the term *monarchy*. Be prepared to help them understand the definition. Remind members that this unit told how Israel became a monarchy.

The Book of Ruth
Have the group open their Bibles to Ruth as you begin the Bible study. Introduce the Book of Ruth by having members describe briefly the basic events of Ruth.

Ask a member to recall the three probable purposes for the Book of Ruth (p. 106):
- to show God's control over history
- to show David's Moabite blood
- to teach Israel to accept returning exiles or foreigners who wished to come and worship with them.

Ask, "Based on our study of the Old Testament to date, what examples of God working in history can you recall?" *(Noah, Abraham, Joseph, Moses, Joshua, and others).* Move to a discussion of how God moves in the lives of His people as individuals and as a church. Help the group see that God acts by placing people in strategic places at the right times.

The Books of 1 and 2 Samuel

Note the Books of Samuel describe how Israel acquired a king, and that they are actually one book in two parts.

Have the members recall the central characters of the Book of 1 Samuel (Samuel, Saul, and David). Note the central character of 2 Samuel is David (p. 108).

Remind members the appearance of a birth narrative in the Scriptures clues us to the importance of the person. Ask a member to recall the events surrounding the birth of Samuel. Be sure to note that Hannah prayed for the child and that she dedicated the child to God.

Help the members see that polygamy was not the ideal, but a response to certain problems in the society. Note the practice cured some problems and caused others. Ask, "What are some problems we find associated with polygamy?" *(Jealousy, rivalry, conflict, partiality, spiteful maneuvering, abuse, and others could be mentioned.)* If the group is slow responding, remind them of Sarah and Hagar (Gen. 16).

Refer members to the activity on page 110 related to the call of Samuel. Use the statements to generate a discussion of his call. Ask members to share which single statement was most significant to them and why.

Events Related to Saul and the Monarchy

Ask the members to recall the reasons the people wanted a king. (They did not trust Samuel's sons, and because they wanted to be like the other nations, p. 112).

Ask, "What was God's view of their request for a king?" (God saw it as rejection of Him).

Then ask members to discuss what happened as a result of the people getting their own way (hardship, 1 Sam. 8:10-18).

Direct a brief discussion to identify Saul's good characteristics. (strength, humility, ability to lead in battle, respected by the people)

The Reasons for Saul's Failure

Divide the group into pairs. Assign the following Scriptures to the pairs. From the following list, assign one reference to each pair. Give the reference only—not the reason for failure. (Depending on group size, each pair may receive two assignments).

- 1 Sam. 13:13-14 (disobeyed God by violating God's law)
- 1 Sam. 14:24-25 (the foolish vow)
- 1 Sam. 15:3,7-9 (failed to destroy plunder taken from the Amalekites)
- 1 Sam. 18:6-9 (He allowed jealousy to control him.)
- 1 Sam. 28:9-10 (He violated his own law.)
- 1 Sam. 31:4-6 (Saul took his own life while fighting the Philistines.)

After five minutes, ask for reports. Allow 10 minutes. Be certain each reason is stated.

Depending on time, engage in discussing the reasons for Saul's failure and the results in his life. You may use the questions interspersed in the following segments.

Discussing the Reasons and Their Results

Read 1 Samuel 13:13-14. Ask, "What are some reasons we sometimes offer to justify disobeying God.What was Samuel's response to Saul? What does that response have to say to us?" (member book, p. 114)

Ask members to discuss their response to the question on page 113. "To what extent does God hold us responsible for foolish promises we have made?" Ask them what the vow revealed to them about Saul.

The activity in the member book, page 114, examines the responses of Saul to the rebuke of Samuel. Refer the group to that activity and ask about their responses.

The Choosing and Anointing of David

Note that at this point God turned from Saul and told Samuel there would be a new leader. Samuel anointed David as Saul's successor. Ask the group if they have any questions related to anointing.

Ask the members to name words describing Saul's attitude toward David. *(You should get words like despised, hated, feared, resented, and others.)*

Saul's encounter with the witch of Endor is a difficult passage. The text states that the witch's contact with Samuel was a hoax. Use the following questions to help members discuss and understand this passage.

a. What were the ways God had chosen to speak to His people? *(Dreams, Urim, through the prophets; 1 Sam. 28:9)*
b. Where was Samuel? *(Where all deceased believers are—with God. Could the witch call him out of heaven?)*
c. Can those who have aligned themselves with evil be trusted to give a true word from God?

There are no easy answers to the questions raised in this passage. If you take the position that God spoke through the witch, how will you convince your fellow Christians not to consult today's mediums and spiritists? I believe that when God has a message for His people, He issues it through one of His own.

The Kingdom of David

What is the term we most often hear to describe David? *(a man after God's own heart)*

Have members turn to the genealogy appearing in Matthew 1. Ask them to take a moment and read verses 1-6. Then ask the following questions:

a. Which names are familiar to you? *(hopefully most of them)*
b. Which names are surprises to you? *(hopefully none)*
c. In what ways does the genealogy seem more interesting after the time you have spent studying the Old Testament?

David and Bathsheba: 2 Samuel 11—12

Have a member recall the events surrounding the episode with Bathsheba. See that members do not overlook the following events in the sequence.

a. Uriah's death (11:14-15).
b. Nathan's rebuke of David (12:1-15). Note that Psalm 51 is thought by most scholars to be David's prayer of confession after the confrontation with Nathan.

Have members turn to the Agree/Disagree statements on page 120. Ask them to share their responses.

The events of David's sin with Bathsheba are some of the best known in the Scriptures. You may choose not to discuss the specifics. However, engage the group in a comparative discussion of Saul and David. Ask, "Why was the kingdom taken from Saul yet David was allowed to keep his position?" The outcome of this discussion could have a bearing on how such problems are dealt with in the church. (The answer lies in the difference of the devotion of their hearts to God, and in the sincerity of their repentance.)

As time permits, discuss the summary statements found on page 121.

CONCLUSION—10 MINUTES

1. Use the two-minute summary you prepared to preview next week's materials. Refer members to the unit learning goals. (No optional assignment this week.)

2. Ask members to share prayer concerns and lead a prayer about those concerns. Then have the members pray a sentence prayer for the person to their left.

After the Session

1. Carefully evaluate the effectiveness of the session. Use the questions that appear on page 14 in the course administrative plan to guide your evaluation.

2. Save any material you have developed for use in future groups of *Step by Step Through the Old Testament.*

3. Immediately begin your preparations for next week's session. Make certain you have learned the memory verses.

4. Pray for the group. This week pray for their understanding of the long-term effects of sin.

GROUP SESSION 8 God and the United and Divided Kingdoms

SESSION GOALS

At the conclusion of this session members will be able to:

1. State the essential facts related to the division of the Monarchy into the Northern and Southern kingdoms.
2. State the essential facts related to the fall of the Northern and Southern kingdoms.
3. State the important dates related to the division of the monarchy.
4. State three applications of the confrontation between Elijah and Ahab at Mt. Carmel.

Before the Session

❑ 1. Study carefully unit 8 and complete all learning activities. Review the group session goals.

❑ 2. Pray for God's guidance as you prepare for this group session. Pray specifically for each member of your group.

❑ 3. Read through "During the Session." Decide on the amount of time to allow for each segment of the Bible study. Write in the margin of your leader guide the time you want each segment to begin.

❑ 4. Prepare a copy of the unit review quiz for each member and gather other materials as needed.

❑ 5. Prepare a two-minute overview of unit 9 to share with the members.

❑ 6. Plan to move your regular seat again this session.

During the Session

Part I
OPENING ACTIVITIES—20 MINUTES

1. Welcome members and begin with prayer. (5 mins.)
2. Memory Review: Have members pair off and quote the memory verses. Participate in this activity with the group. Pair yourself off with a different member each week. (5 mins.)
3. Distribute and have members complete the unit review quiz. When they are finished, lead a discussion of their answers. (10 mins.) Quiz Answers: 1-i; 2-f; 3-g; 4-e; 5-h; 6-b; 7-j; 8-a; 9-c; 10-d.

Part II
BIBLE STUDY AND GROUP DISCUSSION—50 MINUTES

Have group members open their Bibles to 1 Kings as you begin this session.

The Books of Kings and Chronicles
Refer members to the introductory paragraph on page 122. After they have had a moment to look over it, have someone tell the purpose of 1 and 2 Kings.

Note the outline of 1 and 2 Kings. Tell the group the session will follow that outline as they examine the content of this week's study.

Refer the group to the matching activity on page 123. These are the basic facts contained in the review quiz. Go over members' responses and make certain they grasp the basic names, places, and facts related to the division of the kingdom. These are essential to an understanding of the remainder of the Old Testament.

Solomon (1 Kings 1—11)
Ask a member to recount a summary of Solomon's rise to power.

Ask the group to recall the characteristics of Solomon's government. *(large cabinet, heavy taxes, and lots of building projects)*

Refer members to Solomon's address to the people in 1 Kings 8:56-61. Ask, "What stands out as Solomon's most significant statement? What does that have to say to us today?" (member book, p. 128)

Note that even though Solomon started well, he committed sins that cost later generations. Have the group read 1 Kings 11:1-6, which is about Solomon's disobedience. Ask the group to discuss ways our behavior may set the stage for another's downfall. (member book, p. 129)

Have the group continue by reading 1 Kings 11:9-12. Ask, "What reason did God give Solomon for the kingdom being divided and taken from his son?" *(Solomon's sins)*

Ask, "In addition to Solomon's own sin, what other factors seem to have contributed to the division of the kingdom?"

1. Tribal jealousies
2. Solomon's heavy-handed government policies aggravated the tribal hostilities
3. Political ambitions of Jeroboam in the North
4. The foolishness of Solomon's son, Rehoboam

"You cannot follow God today on yesterday's obedience."

The Division of the Kingdom
Ask a member to recall the date the monarchy divided into two kingdoms. *(931 B.C.)*

Call attention to the passage appearing in 1 Kings 12:16-20. Tell the group these few verses record the actual division of the Monarchy. Remind them an understanding of this event is essential to understanding the historical context and the message of the prophets in the Old Testament.

Ask a member to recall the chief sin of the Northern Kingdom *(worship of the golden calves at Dan and Bethel)*. If the group is slow to respond, ask them to turn to 1 Kings 12:28-29 in their Bibles.

Elijah and Ahab: 1 Kings 18
Have the group brainstorm for the facts they can remember about Ahab and Jezebel. Use the true/false activity on page 131 to help them recall the basic facts about these two prominent people.

Activity: For the next activity members will draw out principles or statements of application from the Scripture passage in 1 Kings 18:16-39. Divide the group into three subgroups. Each group will read their assigned passage and prepare a report of it. Allow five minutes for subgroup study and discussion, and ten minutes for reports and large-group discussion.

Subgroup 1—
Verses 16-17: A principle related to how the world sees the church. *(Ahab's accusation of Elijah as the troubler of Israel. The sinful often see the godly as being troublemakers)*

Subgroup 2—
Verse 18: A principle that reveals the reality of why there is hardship, disaster, and ungodliness in the world. *(Elijah's response about the reality of the situation. It is the wicked who bring disaster on a people)*

Subgroup 3—
Verses 30-39: Actions that must take place for true worship, confession, and forgiveness to occur among God's people. *(The rebuilding of the altar symbolized true worship of the Lord by all of His people. Such worship includes prayer, confession, and putting away the causes of ungodliness in our lives)*

This activity may be conducted several ways, depending on the size of your group and the time you have. If you choose not to use subgroups, discuss the passage with the group.

Ask members to share other applications or insights related to this Scripture.

Ask the group to share their responses to the question on page 132 concerning the contest on Mt. Carmel

The Fall of the Northern Kingdom

Summarize this portion for the group. Note for them:

1. There were many kings.
2. All the kings were bent on evil and disobeyed God.
3. There was widespread political instability.
4. The Northern Kingdom was continually assaulted.

Ask a member to recall the reasons for Assyria's policy of deportation. *(to insure no leadership in further revolt against the nation)*

Have members open their books to page 134 and their Bibles to 2 Kings 17:7-8,12-18. After they have a moment to read over the verses, ask them to discuss their responses to the agree/disagree activity. Next, ask them to discuss the reasons they think the Northern Kingdom fell.

The Fall of the Southern Kingdom

Baal Worship. Review or ask a member to share basic facts about Baal worship. Make sure the group understands the terms related to that practice (p. 122). Discuss why this is contrary to God's law. Ask which of the Ten Commandments these practices violated.

Hezekiah and Manasseh

Refer the group to 2 Kings 18:1-8. Ask them what words they used to describe Hezekiah (p. 135). Be sure they make the connection between the reign of Hezekiah and the ministry of the prophet Isaiah.

Contrast the reign of Hezekiah with that of his son Manasseh (2 Kings 21:1-18). You may want to refer to page 136. Ask, "What lessons can we draw from seeing the contrast in Hezekiah and Manasseh?" *(Possible responses are: Good leaders bless the nation, corrupt leaders harm the nation. There is a relationship between the strength to the nation and the moral integrity of the people.)*

Josiah

Ask, "What was King Josiah most noted for?" *(Cleansing the temple, finding and reading the Book of the Law, and the great reform movement around 621 B.C.)* (member book, pp. 136-137)

Judah's Decline and Fall

Note that the death of Josiah at Megiddo also killed the confidence and will of Judah, and that his death seems to be the breaking point in the turn downward for the Southern Kingdom. Ask the group to recall from page 138:

1. The king of Jerusalem's name at the time of the fall. *(Jehoiachin)*
2. The name of the Babylonian king when Judah was carried into captivity. *(Nebuchadnezzar)*
3. The date the captivity began. *(598 B.C.)*
4. The name of the vassal king put on the throne by Nebuchadnezzar. *(Zedekiah)*
5. The reason Nebuchadnezzar attacked Jerusalem. *(Zedekiah's courtship of the Egyptians)*
6. The date the city of Jerusalem fell. *(587 B.C.)*

Consider the unit review on page 138. Make sure the members have the correct responses.

CONCLUSION—10 MINUTES

1. Use the two-minute summary you prepared to preview next week's materials. Refer members to the unit learning goals. Make the following assignment: Walk around the worship and educational facility this week. Think about what it means to you. Why is it special? Where in the buildings have they experienced God? If they had to pick a particular room in which to pray, which would it be?

2. Ask members to share prayer concerns and lead in prayer for those concerns. Then, close in sentence prayer by having the members pray for the person to their right.

After the Session

1. Evaluate the session's effectiveness using the questions on page 14 in the course administrative plan.

2. Save any materials you have developed for use in future groups of *Step by Step Through the Old Testament.*

3. Begin preparation for next week's session. Make certain you have learned the memory verses.

4. Pray for the group to understand God is not limited by time, space, or a particular place in the universe.

GROUP SESSION 9 God and the Exile and Restoration

SESSION GOALS

At the conclusion of this session members will be able to:

1. State one truth each from the lives of Ezra, Nehemiah, and Esther.
2. State the three central elements of Nehemiah's prayer to God.
3. Use the elements of confession, praise, and petition in sentence prayer.

Before the Session

❑ 1. Study carefully unit 9 and complete all learning activities. Review the session goals.

❑ 2. Pray for God's guidance as you prepare for this session. Pray specifically for each member of your group.

❑ 3. Read through "During the Session." Decide on the amount of time to allow for each segment of the Bible study. Make certain you note where follow-up on the affective identification assignment is located. Write in the margin of your leader guide the time you want each segment to begin.

❑ 4. Prepare a copy of the unit review quiz for each member of the group and gather other materials as needed.

❑ 5. Prepare a two-minute overview of the next unit to share with the members.

During the Session

Part I
OPENING ACTIVITIES—20 MINUTES

1. Welcome members and begin with prayer. (5 mins.)
2. Memory Review: Have members pair off and quote the memory verses. Participate in this activity with the group. Pair yourself off with a different member each week. (5 mins.)
3. Distribute and have members complete the unit review quiz. When they are finished, lead a discussion of their answers. Be certain everyone has the correct answers. (10 mins.) Quiz Answers: 1-g; 2-d; 3-c; 4-f; 5-b; 6-j; 7-i; 8-h; 9-a; 10-e.

Part II
BIBLE STUDY AND GROUP DISCUSSION—50 MINUTES

Have participants open their Bibles to the Book of Ezra as you begin this session.

The Books of Ezra and Nehemiah
Note that most scholars believe Ezra authored most of Ezra and Nehemiah, and could have been involved in the authorship of Chronicles. Ask the group what they recall from their study about Ezra (p. 140-141).

Ezra 3:1-5: The Return from the Exile
Ask the group to recall the name of the king who authorized the release from exile. *(Cyrus and Ezra)*

Read Ezra 3:1-5. Ask, "Why do you think the returning Jews first rebuilt the altar?" Allow time for responses. If the group responds slowly, use the following questions to encourage discussion.

1. Why did the kingdom fall? *(the sins of idolatry and rebellion against God, and the sin of accepting the detestable practices of the surrounding peoples)*
2. What was the significance of the altar in this event? *(Rejection of idolatry and a determination to worship only the Lord God)*

Ask the group to recall some of the problems the returning exiles faced. *(hostile neighbors, opposition, threat of conflict, discouragement, unethical business practices)* As you work your way through the selected Scripture passages, you will discover most of the problems that faced the exiles.

Ask members to discuss the way the people who had been left in Palestine treated the returning exiles, and why they felt about them the way they did.

Ezra 4:1-5
Read Ezra 4:1-5. Ask, "What are some frustrations or problems we sometimes encounter in the Christian life?" If this question surfaces problems your members are dealing with, take time to pray a sentence prayer asking God to give them wisdom to deal with the matters. Help the group see that just as God led and blessed Ezra, He can lead and bless them.

Note the author's statements on page 142, "Fourteen years passed without work continuing on the house of the Lord. ... We do know that the people suffered opposition and poverty." Then ask, "Why does conflict seems to hinder progress in God's work?" *(It drains our emotional and spiritual energy, it undermines our motivation, and takes our focus off the Lord's work for us.)*

Ezra 5:1-5
Read Ezra 5:1-5 to see how work began again.
1. Ask the group to state the particular problem that arose. *(opposition from the local governor)*
2. Ask the name of the two prophets God called forth. *(Haggai and Zechariah)*
3. Ask why the people stuck with the task this time. *(Their leaders helped them keep their focus on what God wanted done.)* Ask, "What does this have to say to us?"

The Ministry of Ezra
Note that Ezra comes on the scene in Ezra 7:1. Have the group open their Bibles to Ezra 7:8-10. Ask them the following questions related to the passage.

1. What three things did Ezra commit to do himself? *(study the Word, obey it, and teach it)*
2. What is the progression in the verses?
3. Why is it important to study it and obey it before teaching it?

Allow time for members' discussion. Then ask the group to discuss these questions:

1. What did Jesus ask His disciples to do that He had not done? *(nothing—He never asked them to do anything He had not already done Himself)*
2. If we applied this principle to our teaching in the church, what effect would it have on our church programs?
3. What limitations would this place on our teaching?

Ezra 10:1-17
Note this is one of the more difficult passages in the Old Testament. The command to divorce seems exactly contrary to other Scriptures. Note Ezra's message is not the last word on marriage between God's people and unbelievers. You may refer the group to 1 Corinthians 7:12-16. Remind the group that one principle of interpretation is context. *(historical, grammatical, and literary)* Any passage of Scripture must be seen in both the immediate context and in the wider context of all Scripture.

To summarize this section, ask the group to state truths they have seen in Ezra's example.

The Ministry of Nehemiah
Have the group recall the basic facts about the man Nehemiah and the general story of his ministry.

Read Nehemiah 1:5-11. Have the group pick out the three central elements of Nehemiah's prayer. *(praise, v. 5; confession, vv. 6-7; petition, vv. 8-11)* Ask members to share the order in which they ranked praise, confession, and petition in the activity on page 147 in their books. Then ask, "What did you learn about your prayer life?"

Refer the members to Nehemiah 2:1-20. Recount the basic facts of Nehemiah's return to Jerusalem. As you refer to verses 11-16, ask the group to recall Nehemiah's first actions in Jerusalem. *(He examined the walls and surveyed the damage.)*

Activity: Ask the group to report on their time of reflection this past week. Ask them to respond to these questions:

1. If you came home and found your home in total ruin, how would you feel? If someone hostile to our faith destroyed our worship facilities what would you think?
2. What questions would you ask God? What impact do you think such an event would have on your personal faith?
3. How would you go about rebuilding? *(Members may not choose to respond to all the questions, but do allow time for sharing.)* Summarize by asking, "What do you think Nehemiah felt as he surveyed the walls of Jerusalem?"

Note for the group that Nehemiah was an excellent example for the people. He had a close personal relationship with God, and he was a fair and committed governor. Ask members to discuss why they agree or disagree with this statement: "A person's relationship with God will determine how the person treats other people" (member book, p. 150). Ask them to use examples from their study of Scripture in this course to date to argue their case.

Ask members to share a lesson they drew from the life and ministry of Nehemiah.

The Book of Esther

Have a member tell the basic story of Esther. Be sure she includes the main characters. *(Esther, Mordecai, Haman, King Xerxes)* Be sure group members understand the historical setting. *(in the period during and following the exile)*

Ask a member to recall the uniqueness of the Book of Esther. *(God's name does not appear in it,* member book, p. 152)

Have the group open their Bibles to Esther 4:9-16, and their member books to page 153. Ask them to share their response to Mordecai's argument for Esther to act on behalf of her people. You may ask the following questions:

1. What was the source of Esther's fear?
2. Which argument made the most sense in view of the situation that existed?

Note the annual feast of Purim was established to commemorate the victory God gave through Queen Esther. Ask the members to recall the three main feasts of Judaism. *(Passover, Pentecost, Tabernacles)*

The Messages of Ezra, Nehemiah, and Esther

Read aloud the following truths as outlined in the member's book. As you read them, have the group respond with examples taken from their study of Ezra, Nehemiah, and Esther.

1. God is Lord of History.
2. God is always with His people.
3. The Word of God leads His people to greater faith and spiritual blessings.
4. God's laws affect all of life.
5. God helps His people accomplish their God-given goals.

CONCLUSION—10 MINUTES

1. Pray together. Ask members to pray sentence prayers expressing praise, confession, or a petition to God.

After the Session

1. Carefully evaluate the effectiveness of the session. Use the questions that appear on page 14 in the course administrative plan to guide your evaluation.

2. Save any materials you have developed for use in future groups of *Step by Step Through the Old Testament.*

3. Immediately begin your preparations for next week's session. Make certain you have learned the memory verses.

4. Pray for the group. This week pray for their ability to understand how they can share the truth of God with others.

GROUP SESSION 10 *God and Wisdom*

SESSION GOALS

At the conclusion of this session members will be able to:

1. State the purpose of the Book of Job.

2. Define the Old Testament idea of wisdom.

Before the Session

❑ 1. Study carefully unit 10 and complete all learning activities. Review the session goals.

❑ 2. Pray for God's guidance as you prepare for this session. Pray specifically for each member of your group.

❑ 3. Read through "During the Session." Decide on the amount of time to allow for each segment of the Bible study. Make certain you note where the follow-up on last week's identification assignment is located. Write in the margin of your leader guide the time you want each segment to begin.

❑ 4. Prepare copies of the unit quiz and gather other materials as needed.

❑ 5. Prepare a two-minute overview of the next unit to share with the members.

During the Session

Part I
OPENING ACTIVITIES—20 MINUTES

1. Welcome members and begin with prayer. (5 mins.)

2. Memory Review: Have members pair off and quote the memory verses. Participate in this activity with the group. Pair yourself off with a different member each week. (5 mins.)

3. Distribute and have members complete the unit review quiz. When they are finished, lead a discussion of their answers. Be certain everyone has the correct answers. (10 mins.) Quiz Answers: 1-i; 2-e; 3-f; 4-h; 5-g; 6-a; 7-b; 8-j; 9-c; 10-d.

Part II
BIBLE STUDY AND GROUP DISCUSSION—50 MINUTES

Have group members open their Bibles to the Book of Job as you begin this session.

The Book of Job
As an introduction to the Book of Job, read this question: "What have I done to deserve this?" Ask, "What does such a statement reveal about a person?"

After the discussion, tell the group, "The Book of Job deals with the problem of suffering." Then ask, "What are the three purposes given in your member's book for the writing of Job?" *(Possible answers: to show why good people suffer, to refute the idea that all suffering is a punishment for sin, and to show that God is present with His people in the midst of their suffering,* member book, p. 159). Finally, ask which of the reasons is most important to them and why.

Introduce the matters of setting and writing at this point. Setting refers to and includes historical dates, cultural mores, and other factors in which a story is set or cast. The time of writing is the actual time period, or date, in which the writing occurred. Setting and writing have not always occurred in the same time period.

Ask the group to recall other important facts related to the Book of Job.

Job 4:7-9—Job's Friends
Read Job 4:7-9. Ask, "What was the basic argument of Job's friends?" *(some sin had caused his sorrows)* "What was Job's disposition?" *(he had not sinned)* You may refer them to Job's statement in Job 27:5.

Ask group members what lesson they have learned from this study of Job.

The Book of Psalms
Have the group write in the margin of their books the number of their favorite psalm. Poll the group to learn the different psalms selected. Note duplications and the one or two that seem to be most favored.

Ask the group to recall the two questions that must be considered in determining the authorship of the Psalms (member book, p. 163).

Have the group turn in their books to page 163. Review the structure of Psalms by going over the eight groupings reflected in the outline.

Have the members recall the types of psalms. Ask, "Why do you think people have wanted to put the psalms into categories?" If this proves difficult, then ask how they were helped by seeing them in categories. The answer to the first question should be found as they answer the second question.

Psalm 1
Have the group open their Bibles to Psalm 1. Use the matching activity on page 165 to stimulate the discussion. Ask, "What does the Psalm offer to us?" *(Possible answers: a contrast between the righteous and the wicked, instruction for the righteous for staying right before God)*

Psalm 15
Have the group discuss Psalm 15 using the following questions:

1. What does "walks blamelessly" mean? (v. 2, RSV)

2. What does the phrase "speaks truth from his heart" mean? (v. 2, RSV)

3. What does "keeps his oath even when it hurts" mean? (v. 4, NIV) How does this principle apply to our financial dealings, church commitments, and other matters?

Psalm 103
Have the group turn to Psalm 103 and share their responses to the activity on page 165. Ask, "What three benefits mentioned in the psalm are most precious to you at this time?"

Psalm 137
Have the group open their books to page 167 and read the four facts related to Vengeance Psalms. Ask them to share their response to these questions, "Which of the four facts is most meaningful to you? How did these help you understand such psalms?"

The Book of Proverbs
Ask a member to recall the meaning of the word *proverb. (to compare, or to be like)*

Activity: Have the group develop their own working definition of the Old Testament idea of wisdom. You may refer them to Proverbs 1 for this activity.

Ask the group to recall what they can about the authorship of Proverbs. You may refer them to the activities on page 169 in their books.

Proverbs 15
Ask the group to share the verses in Proverbs 15 that were most significant to them.

Have a member recall the difference between Proverbs and Ecclesiastes. *(Proverbs—optimistic; Ecclesiastes—pessimistic)*

Ecclesiastes

Read Ecclesiastes 1:1. Ask why Solomon is commonly thought to have authored Ecclesiastes. (See p. 170.)

Ask, "What two significant questions are addressed in Ecclesiastes?" *(Is life worth living?* and *What makes life worth living?)*

Ask, "In what circumstances are people still asking these questions today?"

Song of Songs

Read the author's first paragraph related to Song of Songs. Then ask the group to recall the three usual approaches to interpreting the book. *(allegorical, typical, and literal)*

Use the following questions to generate a discussion of how to interpret this book.

1. What is the chief problem with the allegorical method?
2. Why did the author reject the typical method?
3. Why did the author choose the literal method?

Ask the group to share truths they learned in their study this week. Or, if time permits, ask them to share how what they have been studying in *Step by Step Through the Old Testament* has worked its way into other areas of their life.

CONCLUSION—10 MINUTES

1. Use the two-minute summary you prepared to preview next week's materials. Refer members to the unit learning goals.

2. Make the following assignment. Have members watch the media this week for people claiming to have a prophetic message. They will want to compare that person's message with what they learn about God's prophets in the Scripture, and be prepared to share their definition of a prophet in the session next week.

3. Ask members to share prayer concerns and lead in prayer.

After the Session

1. Carefully evaluate the effectiveness of the session. Use the questions that appear on page 14 in the course administrative plan to guide your evaluation.

2. Save any materials you have developed for use in future groups of *Step by Step Through the Old Testament*.

3. Immediately begin your preparations for next week's session. Make certain you have learned the memory verses.

4. Pray for the group. This week pray for their willingness to serve God in a prophetic function whenever they have an opportunity to share the truth of the Scriptures.

5. After this session you will have three more group sessions. Begin thinking about when and how you will conclude this study together. You may want to consider some type celebrative gathering at a member's home for the final session. (If you are using split sessions hold this until three weeks before the group is finished).

GROUP SESSION 11 God and the Major Prophets I

SESSION GOALS

At the conclusion of this session members will be able to:

1. Be able to state the biblical meaning of the word *prophecy*.

2. Have developed a working biblical definition of the role of one who functions as a prophet.

3. Be able to state ways in which Jesus fulfilled the Messianic and Suffering Servant prophecies of Isaiah.

Before the Session

❑ 1. Study carefully unit 11 and complete all learning activities. Review the session goals.

❑ 2. Pray for God's guidance as you prepare for this session. Pray specifically for each member of your group.

❑ 3. Read through "During the Session." Decide on the amount of time to allow for each segment of the Bible study. Make certain you note where the follow-up on last week's identification assignment is located. Write in the margin of your leader guide the time you want each segment to begin.

❑ 4. Prepare and gather the following materials:
- A copy of the unit review quiz for each member.
- Assignment slips with the following emphases of Jeremiah's teaching written on them, one per slip:
  - Inspiration and Revelation, Jeremiah 1:11-16
  - Personal Religion, Jeremiah 20:7-18
  - Sin, Jeremiah 17:5
  - Prayer, Jeremiah 18:18-23
  - Repentance, Jeremiah 4:1-4
  - Externals of Religion, Jeremiah 3:14-18
  - The Individual, Jeremiah 31:29-30
  - The Messiah, Jeremiah 23:5-6
  - The New Covenant, Jeremiah 31:31-34

Prepare enough slips for each member to receive one.

❑ 5. Prepare a two-minute overview of the next unit to share with the members.

During the Session

Part I
OPENING ACTIVITIES—20 MINUTES

1. Welcome members and begin with prayer. (5 mins.)

2. Memory Review: Have members pair off and quote the memory verses. Participate in this activity with the group. Pair yourself off with a different member each week. (5 mins.)

3. Distribute and have members complete the unit review quiz. When they have finished, lead a discussion of their answers. Be certain everyone has the correct answers. (10 mins.) Quiz Answers: 1-a; 2-h; 3-i; 4-b; 5-c; 6-j; 7-d; 8-e; 9-f; 10-g.

Part II
BIBLE STUDY AND GROUP DISCUSSION—50 MINUTES

Have group members open their Bibles to the Book of Isaiah as you begin this session.

The Prophets of the Old Testament
Have the group recall the three parts of the Hebrew Canon. *(Law, Prophets, Writings)*

Have them then recall the five divisions of the English Old Testament. *(Law, History, Wisdom* or *Poetry, Major Prophets, Minor Prophets)*

Start with the person to your right and have members name the Major Prophets. *(Isaiah, Jeremiah, Lamentations, Ezekiel, Daniel)*

Ask, "What is the characteristic that distinguishes the Major Prophets from the Minor Prophets?" *(The length of the books)*

The Nature of Prophecy
Ask a member to describe a biblical prophet. Allow others to add as necessary. (Make notes on this activity.) Lead the group to form a concise working definition that will help them fix in their mind an accurate description of the characteristics and function of the prophet. A possible statement would include, "a person called forth by God to share the truth of God's Word with the people of their day." (Allow 5 mins. for this activity.)

Remind the group that the Eighth Century prophets were Isaiah, Micah, Amos, and Hosea. Then have the group recall the four characteristics of the prophetic message. *(The message comes from God, is rooted in real life, speaks to human nature, and addresses the problem of sin)*

Predictive Prophecy
Activity: Divide the group into three subgroups and assign the following Scriptures:
1. Isaiah 7:3-16
2. Micah 5:1-5
3. Jeremiah 31:27-34

Refer them to the author's answers on page 176 in their books. Give the subgroups five minutes to discuss their assigned passages. Call for reports and use the following questions to guide discussion.
- What was the message for the people of that time?
- What was the historical fulfillment of the prophecy?
- What did this prophecy predict?
- How did people of faith in later times view the passage?

Answers may vary but should reflect the historical principle of interpretation.

The Book of Isaiah: His Call
Read Isaiah 6:1-8. Then ask the group to recall all the information they can about Isaiah and the kings who ruled during Isaiah's ministry. *(Ahaz, Hezekiah, Jotham, Uzziah)*

Help the group recall the three crises that Isaiah faced:
1. Assyrian Crisis: 735-32 B.C. (Isa. 7:1-17)
2. Ashdod Rebellion: 712 B.C. (Isa. 20:1-6)
3. Sennacherib Crisis: 701 B.C. (Isa. 30:15-18)

Ask, "What recent crisis that resulted in a test of Christians' faith immediately comes to mind? How did they respond to it? What did God teach them through it?"

Read Isaiah 31:1-3. Use the following questions to lead a discussion of the passage.
- What is the intent of these verses? *(to encourage trust in God alone)*
- How would you summarize the message of Isaiah the prophet in all three crises?
- What was the "message of that day" for the people of Judah?
- What is the message for us?

Read Isaiah 37:33-38. Use the following questions to lead a discussion of the passage.
- What is God's disposition toward His people in crisis?
- What is the proper response of God's people when faced with crisis?

The Teachings of Isaiah
Ask the group to recall the major teachings from Isaiah studied in this unit. Assign one of these areas to each member of the group. Have members look up the Scripture passage. After a few minutes for reflection have them report one significant insight to the group. (The Messiah/Suffering Servant passages will be done with the entire group.) During the report time you may use the following questions to generate discussion and insight.
1. The Lord's Sovereignty (Isa. 37:21-26)—How can we see God's favor or displeasure expressed in circumstances around us?
2. The Holiness of God (Isa. 6:3)—If we are to be God's Holy people, how can that holiness be expressed in our daily lives?

3. The Doctrine of Sin (Isa. 1:1-4)—How do we spurn God?
4. The Place of Faith (Isa. 12:2-3; 26:3-4)—How does God want us to show our faith in Him?
5. The Doctrine of the Remnant (Isa. 11:11; 37:31-32)—How did the teaching of the remnant offer hope to God's people in Isaiah's day?

The Messianic and Suffering Servant Passages
Ask a member to tell the meaning of the term *Messiah*. If no one recalls the exact meaning, share the meaning with the group. *(The Lord's Anointed Deliverer)*

Time will not permit discussing each passage in detail. You may use the questions below with the selected passage or any of the passages. Or use other discussion questions of your choice. Your purpose will be to help the group see how Jesus fulfilled the Messianic and Suffering Servant teachings in Isaiah.

The Messianic Passages: Isaiah 9:1-7; 11:1-9; 32:1-8
Read Isaiah 11:1-9. Ask the group to respond to the following questions.
- How do you think the teaching of Isaiah gave hope to the people of his day?
- How did you respond to the question in the member's book about whether the word *hopeless* belongs in a Christian's vocabulary?
- What examples from the Gospels fulfill the teaching of Isaiah concerning the Messiah?
- What passages in the Epistles do you recall that interpreted the person and ministry of Christ as the work of the Messiah Isaiah predicted?

The Suffering Servant Passages:
Isaiah 42:1-9; 49:1-6; 50:4-9; 52:13—53:12
Read Isaiah 52:13—53:12. Ask the group to discuss the following questions.
- What examples in the Gospels fulfill the Suffering Servant teaching found in Isaiah?
- What passages do you recall from the Epistles that interpret the person and ministry of Christ as the Suffering Servant of Isaiah's prophecy?

If time permits, ask group members to share any word from the Lord they gained from this unit. (Be sure and save time for assignments for next week's session.)

CONCLUSION—10 MINUTES

1. Use the two-minute summary you prepared to preview next week's materials. Refer members to the unit learning goals.

2. Use the assignment slips you prepared to assign one of the major teachings of the prophet Jeremiah to each member. At the next session members should be prepared to give the group a one-minute summary of the teaching and share one related insight they gained.

3. Indicate to the members the plans for session 13. Ask the group to discuss among themselves the type session they want. They may have to make special arrangements. If they plan some type of social gathering, make certain they include at least an extra hour in the session.

4. Ask members to share prayer concerns and pray together.

After the Session

1. Carefully evaluate the effectiveness of the session. Use the questions that appear on page 14 in the course administrative plan to guide your evaluation.

2. Save any materials you have developed for use in future groups of *Step by Step Through the Old Testament.*

3. Immediately begin your preparations for next week's session. Make certain you have learned the memory verses.

4. Pray for the group. This week pray for their ability to appreciate how God can use diversity in His people to communicate His eternal Word of Truth.

GROUP SESSION 12 *God and the Major Prophets II*

SESSION GOALS

At the conclusion of this session members will be able to:

1. State key passages in the Book of Jeremiah.
2. State an insight from one of the major teachings of Jeremiah.
3. State ways the New Covenant is superior to the Old Covenant.
4. State a lesson from the lives of the major prophets.

Before the Session

❑ 1. Study carefully unit 12 and complete all learning activities. Review the session goals.

❑ 2. Pray for God's guidance as you prepare for this session. Pray specifically for each member of your group.

❑ 3. Read through "During the Session." Decide on the amount of time to allow for each segment of the Bible study. Make certain you note where the follow-up on last week's assignment is located. Write in the margin of your leader guide the time you want each segment to begin.

❑ 4. Prepare and gather the following materials:
- A copy of the Church Growth Study Plan credit request form for each group member. If you copy this for them, then it will not be necessary for them to tear out the one from the back of their member books.
- A copy of the unit review quiz for each member.
- A copy of the following assignment sheet. Duplicate enough copies for each member to have one. Assign one minor prophet to each member.

STUDY ASSIGNMENT AND GUIDELINES

You have been assigned the prophet ___________. As you complete your study this week, spend some extra time on your assigned prophet. Be prepared to report to the group on the following areas in the final session.

1. Meaning of the prophet's name.
2. Primary theme or themes of his message.
3. Historical circumstances, or context, in which he ministered.
4. Reference to one key passage from the study of the book.
5. Probable time period or date of his ministry.
6. One truth or insight gained from his message.

❑ 5. Prepare a two-minute overview of the next unit to share with the members.

❑ 6. Finalize plans for the concluding group session. If you are planning a special event, make certain the group knows the time, place, and what special items (if any) to bring with them.

During the Session

Part I
OPENING ACTIVITIES—20 MINUTES

1. Welcome members and begin with prayer. (5 mins.)

2. Memory Review: Have members pair off and quote the memory verses. Participate in this activity with the group. Pair yourself off with a different member each week. (5 mins.)

3. Distribute and have members complete the unit review quiz. When they are finished, lead a discussion of their answers. Be certain everyone has the correct answers. (10 mins.) Quiz Answers: 1-e; 2-a; 3-b; 4-c; 5-k; 6-i; 7-j; 8-h; 9-d; 10-g; 11-f.

Part II
BIBLE STUDY AND GROUP DISCUSSION—50 MINUTES

Have the group open their Bibles to the Book of Jeremiah as you begin this session.

The Book of Jeremiah
Ask the group to recall significant facts they learned about the Books of Jeremiah and Lamentation.

The content of Jeremiah chapter 36 from the introductory session should be familiar to the group. Ask them to recall how Jeremiah's message came to be written. *(Jeremiah dictated to Baruch.)*

Ask the group to recall from the unit page the chief problem we encounter in understanding the Book of Jeremiah.

The Teachings of Jeremiah
List the emphases to be discussed from the Book of Jeremiah. They are listed here with the Scripture references. Remind members that these teachings and their Scripture references make up the assignments they were to prepare for this session.

- Inspiration and Revelation: Jeremiah 1:11-16
- Personal Religion: Jeremiah 20:7-18
- Sin: Jeremiah 17:5
- Prayer: Jeremiah 18:18-23
- Repentance: Jeremiah 4:1-4
- Externals of Religion: Jeremiah 3:14-18
- The Individual: Jeremiah 31:29-30
- The Messiah: Jeremiah 23:5-6
- The New Covenant: Jeremiah 31:31-34

For this segment, the members will lead the discussion. Give them a moment to look over their notes from their assignment. Have members share with the group a one-minute summary of the particular doctrine and the significant insight they gained from their study. (Try to hold each of the nine reports to three minutes—good luck).

When the report on the Messiah is given, use these questions to expand the discussion.

- Why is the passage considered Messianic in intent?
- How did Jesus fulfill the intent and prophecy of the passage?
- What New Testament passages speak of Jesus' being our Righteousness before God the Father? *(Romans, 2 Corinthians)*

When the report on the new covenant is given, use the following questions to expand the discussion.

- What were the characteristics of the Old Covenant? *(law written on tablets of stone, broken covenant, and mediated by priests and prophets)*
- In what ways was the new covenant to be superior to the old covenant? *(First, the law would be written on the hearts of individuals. Second, the new covenant would*

mark a new relationship between God and His people. Third, all classes of people would know the Lord.)

Take about five minutes and summarize the Book of Jeremiah using the information from the member's book. Be sure to include that Jeremiah ministered during the traumatic period of the fall of the Southern Kingdom, and that he was never accepted by the people to whom he prophesied. Include other facts you sense will help the group understand Jeremiah. Note the author's statement that "for Jeremiah success meant following God even when others refused to do so" (member book, p. 193).

The Book of Lamentations
Refer the group to page 191 in their member books. Have them read over the section that tells about the authorship and date of Lamentations. Ask whether they have any questions.

Ask, "What is the uniqueness of the structure of Lamentations?" *(Written in five dirges or funeral songs).*

Ask the group to recall the meaning of the term *Lamentation.*

Ask group members to share the chapter of Lamentations they chose to read.

The Book of Ezekiel
Read Ezekiel 1:1-3 to the group and ask the group to share their responses to the following questions.

- When did the prophet Ezekiel experience his call to minister? *(Around age 30, in exile in Babylon)*

- What do you see in a comparison of the ministries of Jeremiah and Ezekiel? *(Jeremiah prophesied in Judah before and during the fall of the Southern Kingdom. Ezekiel prophesied to the exiles in Babylon prior to and after the fall of Jerusalem. Note that even in exile, God did not leave His people without His word of comfort, guidance, and correction.)*

Have the group recall the basic facts about Ezekiel the man. *(Son of Buzi the priest, called at age 30, ministered for 22 years, acted out a dramatic message, used his life circumstances to communicate the message of God)*

State that several years ago Marshall McCluhan, a communications theorist, introduced the concept that the way a message is delivered is actually the message. Then use these questions to lead a discussion of the way Jeremiah delivered his message.

- Why would you say Ezekiel beat McCluhan to the idea that the messenger is the message? *(Examples: 4:1-8; 24:15-17)*

- What does this idea mean in day-to-day terms?

- What does it have to say to us as Christians?

Your purpose here is to help the group see that God can use the events of our lives to speak to others and that we indeed have a life-message that is rooted in our relationship to God.

Note the summary of Ezekiel's preaching beginning on page 202.

1. Ezekiel was called to be a watchman over God's people (Ezek. 3:16-19).

2. Ezekiel emphasized the sovereignty of God (Ezek. 11:1-9).

3. Ezekiel developed the concept of individual responsibility (Ezek. 18:1-20).

4. Ezekiel gave hope for the future (Ezek. 11:17-21).

The Book of Daniel
Ask the group to state briefly the three major views of interpreting Daniel. *(1. It pictures the second coming of Christ; 2. It describes events of the second century B.C.; 3. It looks forward to the coming kingdom of God in the person of Jesus Christ.)*

Have the group turn to the activity on page 203 in their books. Ask, "Which account did you choose to read? What do you think is the major message for today in the particular passage of Scripture?"

CONCLUSION—10 MINUTES

1. Use the two-minute summary you prepared to preview next week's materials. Refer members to the unit learning goals. Make the following assignment. All members are to complete the unit on the minor prophets. Each member will be assigned one or more of the 12 to report on.

Their assignment is to be prepared to report to the group:

a. The meaning of the prophet's name.

b. The primary theme or themes of his message.

c. The historical context.

d. The reference to one key passage from the study of the book.

e. The probable time period or date of his ministry.

f. One truth or insight they gained from his message.

2. Give each member a copy of the course credit request form. Instruct the members to complete these this week and bring back to the concluding session.

3. If you have not already done so, announce the final plans for the concluding group session.

4. Ask members to share their prayer concerns and pray together.

After the Session

1. Carefully evaluate the effectiveness of the session. Use the questions that appear on page 14 in the course administrative plan to guide your evaluation.

2. Save any materials you have developed for use in future groups of *Step by Step Through the Old Testament.*

3. Immediately begin your preparations for next week's session. Make certain you have learned the memory verses.

4. Pray for the group. This week pray for their recall of the significant truths of God that have been revealed to them in their walk with Him as they have studied *Step by Step Through the Old Testament.*

GROUP SESSION 13 God and the Minor Prophets

SESSION GOALS

At the conclusion of this session members will be able to:

1. State the three major interpretations of Hosea's marriage.

2. State the themes from the messages of the minor prophets.

3. State the location and probable dates of each prophet's ministry.

4. State one insight or application from the message of an assigned prophet.

5. Give a testimony of spiritual growth as a result of the study of the Old Testament.

Before the Session

❑ 1. Study carefully unit 13 and complete all learning activities. Review the session goals.

❑ 2. Pray for God's guidance as you prepare for this session. Pray specifically for each group member.

❑ 3. Read through "During the Session." Decide on the amount of time to allow for each segment of the Bible study. The amount of content in this unit will make it impossible to cover it all thoroughly. Decide beforehand how you want to focus on the segments. There are two options for conducting the Bible study segment in this unit.

Option 1: Use the reports made by the group members as the basis for introducing the Bible study. Let the discussion questions flow naturally out of the content. Use the suggested questions in the leader guide for follow-up discussion after the reports are finished.

Option 2: Follow the leader guide in order, calling for the different reports as you get to that prophet. If you choose this option, make sure you stay on track and cover everyone's report. If you are in doubt, choose option 1. Write in the margin of your leader guide the time you want each segment to begin.

❑ 4. Gather the following materials:
- A copy of the unit review quiz for each member.
- Enough three-by-five-inch cards for each member to have one.

❑ 5. Contact your host, if you are meeting in a home, to make certain all is in order for the concluding session. If the host needs assistance, enlist group members to help you with necessary preparations.

During the Session

Part I
OPENING ACTIVITIES—20 MINUTES

1. Welcome members and begin with prayer. (5 mins.)

2. Memory Review: Have members pair off and quote the memory verses. Review your Scriptures with a member you have not worked with before. (5 mins.)

3. Distribute and have members complete the unit review quiz. When they have finished, lead a discussion of their answers. Be certain everyone has the correct answers. (10 mins.) Quiz Answers: 1-c; 2-e; 3-i; 4-l; 5-g; 6-a; 7-f; 8-k; 9-j; 10-h; 11-d; 12-b.

Part II
BIBLE STUDY AND GROUP DISCUSSION—50 MINUTES

Have the group open their Bibles to the Book of Hosea as you begin this session.

The Book of Hosea

Have the group recall the basic facts they remember about the prophet Hosea.

Ask, "Which prophets were contemporaries of Hosea?" *(Isaiah, Amos, Micah)*

Ask where the four prophets ministered. *(Isaiah and Micah in the Southern Kingdom, Amos and Hosea in the Northern Kingdom)*

Refer the members to their member books on pages 207-208, the theories concerning Hosea's wife. Ask, "Were you aware of the moral problem of this passage prior to this study of the Old Testament?"

Ask the group to recall the three interpretations of Hosea's marriage offered by the author.

1. Allegorical: The names and places are not literal but symbolic, representing spiritual truths.
2. Literal: God spoke to Hosea and told him to marry a harlot.
3. Literal/Looking Back: Hosea looked back on a tragic marriage and saw God's message for unfaithful Israel in his own circumstances.

Ask, "Which view do you feel is most sound? Why?" Allow the group to discuss this. Then ask, "Do you think Hosea should have been disqualified from being a prophet because of his wife?" (See what the discussion brings. If they say yes, ask, "What counsel do you think King David would give?" *Obviously, God did not disqualify Hosea, even though most people would.)*

The Books of Joel and Amos

Use the following questions to guide a discussion of the implications of the locust plague in Joel 2:1-11.

- What had caused the plague? *(The sin of the people)*
- How would such a plague affect an agricultural economy?
- How would such a plague alter daily patterns or one's standard of living?
- What could be done to avert it?

Use the following questions to lead the group to interpret some of what they have read.

- Can we see the hand of God behind similar circumstances in our community, nation, or the world?
- What specific circumstances come to your mind?
- What do you think God is saying to us?
- How should we respond as individuals, as a church, as a nation?

Have the group open their Bibles to the Book of Amos. Ask them to recall what they can about this prophet.

Ask, "Which themes characterized the message of Amos?" *(He preached concerning the excesses of the wealthy, and against the superficial worship of the people.)*

Read Amos 2:6-8,12. Have the group record in the margin of their books the sins mentioned in the verses. Ask them to share their responses to these questions.

- What types of people were involved in these things? *(God's people)*
- Where have you seen these same sins today?
- What does this have to say to us?

The Books of Obadiah and Jonah

Ask, "What was Obadiah's primary message?" *(Condemnation of those taking pleasure in their neighbors' hardship)*

Ask, "What's your first thought when I say *Jonah?*" Refer the group to the author's paragraph on page 213. Read the sentence, "Jonah did not want God to forgive the people of Nineveh. He wanted God to condemn them." Ask the group to discuss their responses to these questions.

- What do you think of such an attitude?
- What evidences do you see that such attitudes may still be with us?
- How do you think God feels about it?
- What does this have to say to what we do in our church, community, or nation as a result of knowing God's will?

Ask, "What new truths did you get from your studying Jonah?"

The Book of Micah

Ask the group to recall the theme of Micah's message. *(Performing acts of justice and mercy and thus fulfilling the demands of God's covenant relationship)*

The Books of Nahum, Habakkuk, Zephaniah, Haggai, Zechariah, and Malachi

Call for members' reports to cover the content of these prophetic books.

Optional: A Summary of the Prophetic Message

No summary is ever complete or inclusive of all the teachings of the Scriptures. God's Word is eternal, unchanging, and complete. It speaks with an eloquence and rings with an authority humanity's word will never have. However, in seeking to understand His Word, we benefit from categories, summaries, and outlines.

The following are several key themes appearing many times in the messages of all the prophets. In summarizing the minor prophets for the group, read the statement and ask the group to recall passages that illustrate that teaching. Their references may come from anywhere in the Old Testament. A reference is listed in case group members have difficulty recalling.

God loves His people. (Hos. 14:4)
God hates sin. (Jer. 44:4,21-22)
God judges His people. (Jer. 2:35)
God forgives His people. (Hos. 14:2,4)
God loves all people. (Jonah 4:10-11)
God is present with His people. (Zeph. 3:15)
God gives hope to His people in all circumstances. (Mal. 4:1-3)
God expects His people to honor Him by living His word with integrity. (Amos 5:24; Mic. 6:8)

Optional Activity: Give three-by-five-inch cards to the members. Ask them to reflect for a few minutes on the things God has said to them over the past 13 sessions and to record their reflections. Use the following questions to guide their thinking. You also may want to use the following questions in this discussion:

- Who was the most notable character you studied?
- What was the most surprising thing you learned?
- What one truth has God been using to adjust your life to His agenda?
- How has God been using the growth in your life to enable you to serve Him more effectively?

Ask for volunteers to share what they recorded.

CONCLUSION—30 MINUTES

1. Take up the course credit request forms. Make certain they are filled out properly before you go to the next activity.

2. Take up the course evaluations. Place them in your leader guide for later reading.

3. Ask members to share prayer concerns and pray together. You should pray last. Ask the Lord to use the growth that has occurred in the group members' lives to honor and magnify His name in the church and community in which you all live.

After the Session

1. Carefully evaluate the effectiveness of the session. Use the questions that appear on page 14 in the course administrative plan to guide your evaluation.

2. Save any materials you have developed for use in future groups of *Step by Step Through the Old Testament.*

3. Make contact with members who expressed an interest in leading future groups of *Step by Step Through the Old Testament.* Make yourself available to answer questions and to serve as a resource person to them should they accept the task.

4. Pray for the group. In your concluding personal prayer for them, pray for their commitment to continue to walk daily with God by abiding in Christ.

5. Make certain the Christian Growth diploma forms are mailed to the Christian Growth Study Plan; 127 Ninth Avenue, North; Nashville, TN 37234-0117. Alert the person receiving your church mail that the diplomas will be coming. Be certain the members receive the diplomas and other recognition as appropriate.

UNIT REVIEW QUIZZES

UNIT 1 REVIEW QUIZ

A. Match the name on the left with the correct answer on the right. Fill in the blank with the correct letter.

____ 1. Jebusites	A. Villagers/central Palestine
____ 2. Perizzites	B. Inhabitants of the land west of the Jordan River
____ 3. Hittites	C. Inhabitants of Jerusalem
____ 4. Canaanites	D. North of Palestine
____ 5. Egyptians	E. From between the Tigris and Euphrates Rivers
____ 6. Syrians	F. From Turkey in the Central Hill Country
____ 7. Babylonians	G. Used Palestine as a buffer zone
____ 8. Assyrians	H. East of the Dead Sea
____ 9. Edomites	I. Southwestern part of Palestine
____ 10. Moabites	J. Northern coast of Palestine
____ 11. Ammonites	K. East of the Jordan River
____ 12. Philistines	L. South of Palestine
____ 13. Phoenicians	M. At the mouth of the Tigris and Euphrates Rivers

B. Fill in the blanks to name the Principles of Interpretation.

Determine the K______________________ ______________ L______________________

Determine the C____

Determine the H______________________ S ______________________

Determine the G______________________ M ______________________

Determine Your Own S______________________ C ______________________

- -

UNIT 2 REVIEW QUIZ

A. Match the statement on the left with the correct answer on the right. Fill in the blank with the correct letter.

___ 1. The Beginnings and the Patriarchs	A. Genesis 4
___ 2. Means "Five Books"	B. Genesis 11:1-9
___ 3. To have intellect, emotions, and a will	C. Two periods of Old Testament history covered in Genesis
___ 4. The focus of Genesis 1	D. Creation of the universe
___ 5. The focus of Genesis 2	E. The Hebrew word *bara*
___ 6. The fall of humanity	F. Being in the image of God
___ 7. Cain and Abel	G. Pentateuch
___ 8. The Flood passages	H. Genesis 6—9
___ 9. The Tower of Babel	I. The creation of humanity
___10. Used only of God in the Old Testament	J. Genesis 3

B. Fill in the blanks to complete the five divisions of the English Old Testament.

L____

H____

W______________________ or P ______________________

M______________________ P ______________________

M______________________ P ______________________

UNIT 3 REVIEW QUIZ

A. Match the statement on the left with the correct answer on the right. Fill in the blank with the correct letter.

____ 1. Left Ur of the Chaldees together	A. Genesis 32
____ 2. The call of Abraham	B. Jacob
____ 3. The son of Abraham and Sarah's handmaid	C. Esau
____ 4. God's covenant with Abraham	D. Ishmael
____ 5. The brother of Jacob	E. Abraham and Sarah
____ 6. The near sacrifice of Isaac	F. Genesis 12:1-5
____ 7. The son of Isaac	G. Joseph
____ 8. The son of Abraham and Sarah	H. Isaac
____ 9. Jacob's encounter with God	I. Genesis 15; 17
____ 10. The son of Jacob	J. Genesis 22:1-18

B. Fill in the blanks to complete the Principles of Interpretation.

Determine the K ______________________________ of L ______________________________

Determine the C ______________________________

Determine the H ______________________________ S ______________________________

Determine the G ______________________________ M ______________________________

Determine your own S ______________________________

C. Fill in the blanks to complete the list of the books of the Law.

G ______________________________

E ______________________________

L ______________________________

N ______________________________

D ______________________________

- -

UNIT 4 REVIEW QUIZ

A. Match the statement on the left with the correct answer on the right. Fill in the blank with the correct letter.

____ 1. Moses' big mistake	A. Sheep herder
____ 2. The birth narrative of Moses	B. Killed an Egyptian
____ 3. Moses' father-in-law	C. Aaron
____ 4. The call of Moses	D. Exodus 6—12
____ 5. Moses' occupation in Midian	E. Exodus 3—4
____ 6. The plague passages	F. Jethro
____ 7. God spoke to Moses	G. Mountain of God
____ 8. The account of the Exodus	H. Burning bush
____ 9. Horeb	I. Exodus 2:1-10
____ 10. Moses' brother	J. Exodus 13:5-22

B. Write from memory the five divisions of the English Old Testament.

____

____

____

____

____

C. Write from memory the five books of the Law.

____

____

____

____

____

UNIT 5 REVIEW QUIZ

A. Match the statement on the left with the correct answer on the right. Fill in the blank with the correct letter.

____ 1. The central chapter of the Book of Exodus
____ 2. Leviticus
____ 3. The Ten Commandments
____ 4. The central chapter of Leviticus
____ 5. The first four commandments
____ 6. The Day of Atonement
____ 7. The last six commandments
____ 8. The Book of Numbers
____ 9. It symbolized the presence of God with His people
____ 10. To form a relationship

A. Covenant
B. Records the wilderness wanderings of the nations of Israel
C. Israel confessed their sin and sought God's forgiveness
D. Leviticus 16
E. Answers the question of how sinful people can come into the presence of Holy God
F. Exodus 20
G. Our relationship with God
H. Exodus 19
I. Relate to how we get along with others
J. Tabernacle

B. Fill in the blanks to complete the Principles of Interpretation.

Determine the K ____________________ of L ____________________
Determine the C ____________________
Determine the H ____________________ S ____________________
Determine the G ____________________ M ____________________
Determine your own S ____________________ C ____________________

- -

UNIT 6 REVIEW QUIZ

A. Match the statement on the left with the correct answer on the right. Fill in the blank with the correct letter.

____ 1. The conquest of the land
____ 2. The Feast of Tabernacles
____ 3. The division of the land
____ 4. The Feast of Pentecost
____ 5. Succeeded Moses as leader of the nation
____ 6. The Feast of Passover
____ 7. She hid the spies
____ 8. God's election of Israel
____ 9. His sin caused Israel's defeat of Ai
____ 10. The Shema

A. Also the Feast of Weeks, it came after the first barley harvest
B. Celebrated sparing Israel's children the night the firstborn of all Egypt were killed
C. Joshua
D. Joshua 13—24
E. Rahab
F. Deuteronomy 7
G. Also the Feast of Booths. It reenacted the Israelites' journey in the wilderness
H. Achan
I. Deuteronomy 6:4-9
J. Joshua 1-12

B. Fill in the blanks to complete the list of the books of history.

J ____________________ C ____________________
J ____________________ E ____________________
R ____________________ N ____________________
S ____________________ E ____________________
K ____________________

UNIT 7 REVIEW QUIZ

A. Match the statement on the left with the correct answer on the right. Fill in the blank with the correct letter.

____ 1. This woman was a native of the land of Moab	A. War in his own family
____ 2. To be set apart for special service	B. Saul
____ 3. She was bitter over the death of her husband and sons	C. 1 and 2 Samuel
____ 4. The anointing of David	D. 1 Samuel 16:1-13
____ 5. The most well known of Ruth's descendants	E. Ruth
____ 6. The primary reason Saul failed	F. Naomi
____ 7. Books that describe how Israel acquired a king	G. Disobedience to God
____ 8. Passages telling of the choice of Saul	H. Samuel
____ 9. He served as a judge, priest, and prophet	I. 2 Samuel 11
____ 10. The first king of Israel	J. 1 Samuel 9—11
____ 11. David and Goliath	K. 1 Samuel 17
____ 12. David and Bathsheba	L. David
____ 13. The result of David's sin	M. Anoint

B. Fill in the blanks to complete the Principles of Interpretation.

Determine the K ______________________ of L ______________________

Determine the C ______________________

Determine the H ______________________ S ______________________

Determine the G ______________________ M ______________________

Determine your own S ______________________ C ______________________

C. Fill in the blanks to complete the list of the books of history.

J ______________________	C ______________________
J ______________________	E ______________________
R ______________________	N ______________________
S ______________________	E ______________________
K ______________________	

- -

UNIT 8 REVIEW QUIZ

A. Match the statement on the left with the correct answer on the right. Fill in the blank with the correct letter.

____ 1. Date the nation of Israel was divided into two kingdoms	A. Josiah
____ 2. Date of the fall of Jerusalem	B. Judah
____ 3. Capital of the Northern Kingdom	C. Nebat
____ 4. Capital of the Southern Kingdom	D. 722 B.C.
____ 5. Another name for the Northern Kingdom	E. Jerusalem
____ 6. Another name for the Southern Kingdom	F. 587 B.C.
____ 7. Kings who served God faithfully	G. Samaria
____ 8. Proved to be Judah's best king	H. Israel
____ 9. The father of Jeroboam	I. 931 B.C.
____ 10. Date Samaria fell to Assyria	J. Hezekiah and Josiah

B. Fill in the blanks to complete from memory the list of the books of history.

______________________	______________________
______________________	______________________
______________________	______________________
______________________	______________________
______________________	______________________

UNIT 9 REVIEW QUIZ

A. Match the statement on the left with the correct answer on the right. Fill in the blank with the correct letter.

____ 1. These books describe people who lived in difficult times	A. Nehemiah
____ 2. These two books are believed to have been written by the same author	B. Cyrus
____ 3. Setting for the Book of Esther	C. Persian city of Susa
____ 4. Beginning of Ezra's known ministry	D. Ezra and Nehemiah
____ 5. The Persian king who allowed the Jews to return from exile	E. Artaxerxes
____ 6. A shortened word to identify a person who is from Judea	F. 485 B.C.
____ 7. The year the Jews were allowed to return from the exile	G. Ezra, Nehemiah, Esther
____ 8. Restored proper worship practice to the Jews	H. Ezra
____ 9. Led in the rebuilding of the walls of Jerusalem	I. 536 B.C.
____ 10. King who released Nehemiah to carry out his ministry	J. Jew

B. Fill in the blanks to complete the Principles of Interpretation.

Determine the K ______________________________ of L ______________________________

Determine the C ______________________________

Determine the H ______________________________ S ______________________________

Determine the G ______________________________ M ______________________________

Determine your own S ______________________________ C ______________________________

Write from memory the five divisions of the English Old Testament.

____

____

____

____

____

- -

UNIT 10 REVIEW QUIZ

A. Match the statement on the left with the correct answer on the right. Fill in the blank with the correct letter.

____ 1. Old Testament book that is a series of love poems	A. Psalms
____ 2. This question reflects the meaning of wisdom.	B. Solomon
____ 3. Division of the Hebrew Old Testament in which the wisdom literature appears	C. A proverb
____ 4. Old Testament book that deals with the problem of suffering	D. Ecclesiastes
____ 5. Receives credit for much of the Book of Psalms	E. How can I live the best life possible?
____ 6. Content of this book expresses the deep, innermost feelings of people's hearts	
____ 7. Ecclesiastes is commonly thought to be authored by this man.	F. Writings
____ 8. This book is basically optimistic and relates wisdom to daily life.	G. David
____ 9. A comparison	H. Job
____ 10. Book that is essentially pessimistic	I. Song of Songs
	J. Proverbs

B. Write from memory the Old Testament books of Wisdom.

____

____

____

____

____

UNIT 11 REVIEW QUIZ

A. Match the statement on the left with the correct answer on the right. Fill in the blank with the correct letter.

____ 1. These books are called the major prophets because of the length of their message.
____ 2. Nature of true biblical prophecy
____ 3. Books called the minor prophets because of the length of their message
____ 4. Messianic passages in the Book of Isaiah
____ 5. People who proclaimed God's Word to their own generations
____ 6. Suffering servant poems in Isaiah
____ 7. Eighth century B.C. prophets
____ 8. One of the faithful kings during the time of Isaiah's ministry
____ 9. Scriptural account of Isaiah's call experience
____ 10. An event marking the time when Isaiah's ministry began

A. Isaiah, Jeremiah, Ezekiel, Daniel
B. Isaiah 9:1-7; 56:1-8
C. The prophets
D. Isaiah, Micah, Amos, Hosea
E. Hezekiah
F. Isaiah 6:1-8
G. Following the death of King Uzziah
H. Spoke the truth of God to people
I. Hosea, Joel, Amos, Obadiah, Jonah, Micah, Nahum, Habakkuk, Zephaniah, Haggai, Zechariah, Malachi
J. Isaiah 42:1-9; 49:1-6; 52:13—53:12

B. Fill in the blanks to complete the Principles of Interpretation.

Determine the K ______________________ of L ______________________
Determine the C ______________________
Determine the H ______________________ S ______________________
Determine the G ______________________ M ______________________
Determine your own S ______________________ C ______________________

C. Go back and underline, repeating to yourself, the names of the major prophets.

D. Go back and circle, repeating to yourself, the names of the minor prophets.

UNIT 12 REVIEW QUIZ

A. Match the statement on the left with the correct answer on the right. Fill in the blank with the correct letter.

____ 1. Most fateful 50-year period in Israel's history
____ 2. Statesman prophet comfortable with royalty
____ 3. Accepted dates of Jeremiah's ministry
____ 4. A dirge or funeral song
____ 5. Jeremiah's definition of sin
____ 6. Jeremiah's favorite designation for the Messiah
____ 7. Primary Messianic passages in Jeremiah
____ 8. The New Covenant passage in Jeremiah
____ 9. Longest Old Testament quotation found in the New Testament
____ 10. A small-town prophet rejected by the nation
____ 11. A priestly prophet with a unique personality

A. Isaiah
B. 626-587 B.C.
C. Lamentation
D. Hebrews 8:8-12
E. 625-575 B.C.
F. Ezekiel
G. Jeremiah
H. Jeremiah 31:31-34
I. Righteous branch
J. Jeremiah 23:5-6
K. To turn one's heart away from God

B. Write from memory the names of the Major Prophets.

____
____
____
____

UNIT 13 REVIEW QUIZ

A. Match the statement on the left with the correct answer on the right. Fill in the blank with the correct letter.

____ 1. The Lord used the heartbreak of marital problems to speak through this prophet.
____ 2. Hosea 14:2,4
____ 3. This prophet is quoted extensively by Simon Peter at Pentecost in Acts 2.
____ 4. These prophets ministered to the returning exiles in Jerusalem
____ 5. Prophet who issued a strong condemnation of the superficial worship of affluent, selfish people
____ 6. Shortest book in the Old Testament
____ 7. This prophet was more concerned with his personal prejudices and physical comfort than for the people to whom God called him to preach.
____ 8. Eighth century B.C. prophets who prophesied in the Southern Kingdom
____ 9. Eighth century B.C. prophets who prophesied in the Northern Kingdom
____ 10. Micah 6:8
____ 11. Minor prophets who were contemporaries of the prophet Isaiah
____ 12. Zephaniah 3:15

A. Obadiah
B. "The LORD has taken away your punishment, he has turned back your enemy. The LORD, the King of Israel, is with you; never again will you fear any harm."
C. Hosea
D. Hosea, Amos, Micah
E. "Take words with you and return to the LORD. Say to him: 'Forgive all our sins and receive us graciously, that we may offer the fruit of our lips.' " "I will heal their waywardness and love them freely, for my anger has turned away from them."
F Jonah
G. Amos
H. "He has showed me, O man, what is good. And what does the LORD require of you? To act justly and to love mercy and to walk humbly with your God."
I. Joel
J. Hosea and Amos
K. Isaiah and Micah
L. Haggai and Zechariah

B. Write from memory the Principles of Interpretation.

____
____
____
____
____

C. Write from memory the names of the Minor Prophets.

____________________ ____________________
____________________ ____________________
____________________ ____________________
____________________ ____________________
____________________ ____________________

What is *Step by Step Through the Old Testament?*

Step by Step Through the Old Testament is an intensive discipleship training course covering the 39 books of the Old Testament. It is designed to equip church program teachers and other church members with the skills and knowledge necessary to interpret and apply the Old Testament Scriptures to their Christian experience. The course is made up of 13 units covering the following subject areas:

The Old Testament Revelation
The Creation
The Patriarchs
The Exodus (Part I)
The Exodus (Part II)
The Land of Promise
The Beginning of the Monarchy
The United and Divided Kingdoms
The Exile and Restoration
God and Wisdom
The Major Prophets (Part I)
The Major Prophets (Part II)
The Minor Prophets

What Will Be Expected of Me?
Participants will be expected to learn selected memory verses related to the subject matter of each unit. You will need to devote an average of 30 minutes per day to Bible study and preparation. Once each week you will meet for a two-hour group session with other group members.

How Do I Get Involved?
You have been prayerfully enlisted for this course. Please give your thoughtful consideration to being a part of *Step by Step Through the Old Testament*. Plan to come to the get-acquainted session to hear more. A get acquainted session is scheduled for:

Date and Time: **Place:**

Unit 1—God and His Revelation

2 Timothy 3:16
All Scripture is God-breathed and is useful for teaching, rebuking, correction and training in righteousness.
—2 Timothy 3:16, NIV

Unit 2—God's Creation of Man

John 1:3
Through him all things were made; without him nothing was made that has been made.
—John 1:3, NIV

Unit 3—God's Call to Abraham

Galatians 3:6
Consider Abraham: "He believed God, and it was credited to him as righteousness."
—Galatians 3:6, NIV

Unit 4—God Redeems His people

Exodus 14:13a
"Do not be afraid. Stand firm and you will see the deliverance the LORD will bring you today."
—Exodus 14:13a, NIV

Unit 5—God's Covenant With His People

Exodus 19:5-6
"If you obey me fully and keep my covenant, then out of all nations you will be my treasured possession. Although the whole earth is mine, you will be for me a kingdom of priests and a holy nation."
—Exodus 19:5-6, NIV

Unit 6—The Shame

Deuteronomy 6:4-5
Hear, O Israel: The LORD our God, the LORD is one. Love the LORD your God with all your heart and with all your soul and with all your strength.
—Deuteronomy 6:4-5, NIV

Unit 7—The Heart

1 Samuel 16:7b
"The LORD does not look at the things man looks at. Man looks at the outward appearance, but the LORD looks at the heart."
—1 Samuel 16:7b, NIV

Unit 8—Hezekiah's Prayer

2 Kings 19:15a
"O LORD, God of Israel, enthroned between the cherubim, you alone are God over all the kingdoms of the earth."
—2 Kings 19:15a, NIV

Unit 9—God Restores His People

Ezra 3:11a
With praise and thanksgiving they sang to the LORD:
"He is good;
his love to Israel endures forever."
—Ezra 3:11a, NIV

Unit 10—God Gives Wisdom

Proverbs 2:1,5-6
My son, if you accept my words and store up my commands within you … then you will understand the fear of the LORD and find the knowledge of God. For the LORD gives wisdom, and from his mouth come knowledge and understanding.
—Proverbs 2:1,5-6, NIV

Unit 11—The Prophet's Message: God's Faithfulness

Lamentations 3:22-23
Because of the Lord's great love we are not consumed, for his compassions never fail. They are new every morning; great is your faithfulness.
—Lamentations 3:22-23, NIV

Unit 12—The Prophet's Message: Repentance

Hosea 14:1
Return, O Israel, to the LORD your God.
Your sins have been your downfall!
—Hosea 14:1, NIV

Unit 13—The Prophet's Message: Hope

Isaiah 9:2
The people walking in darkness have seen a great light; on those living in the land of the shadow of death a light has dawned.
—Isaiah 9:2, NIV